the doctrine of MAN

William L. Hendricks

CONVENTION PRESS
Nashville, Tennessee

5133-16

This book is the text for a course
in the subject area Baptist Doctrine
in the Church Study Course

Credits:
Art: *The Creation* by Michelangelo, Courtesy of the Bettman Archive. Photographs: *Girl At Window,* Nancy Arnold; *Boy Reading, Family Worshiping, Woman At Desk,* Dan Lofton; *Carton,* Doug Brachey; *Father and Daughters,* Jack Corn/Image.
Design and format by Haskell D. Richardson.
Manuscript assistant: Anne Donahue

Dewey Decimal Classification Number: 233
Subject: MAN

Printed in the United States of America

About the Author

Since 1957, William L. Hendricks has been professor of theology at Southwestern Baptist Theological Seminary. Dr. Hendricks, a native of Montana, is a graduate of Oklahoma Baptist University (A.B.) and Southwestern Baptist Theological Seminary (B.D.). He also holds an M.A. and a Ph.D. from University of Chicago.

Dr. Hendricks is no stranger to those who are regular readers of Southern Baptist materials. He has appeared regularly as the author of articles in numerous publications. *The Doctrine of Man* joins *Tapestries of Truth* which he authored and *Resource Unlimited* which he edited.

Dr. Hendricks and his wife Lois Ann have one son John Lawrence.

Contents

Three Ways to Study This Book

LARGE GROUP STUDY

This book is the text for Baptist Doctrine Study 1978. Most of the studies will be conducted in groups of twenty-five or more. These large group sessions will be more effective if the leader will adapt the small group study guides for use by a larger group and use the teaching aids in the *Baptist Doctrine Study 1978 Teaching and Promotion Kit—Man* (Item 5143-16 on the Undated Materials Order Form).

SMALL GROUP STUDY

Church Training groups or other small groups can study this book by using the directions for leading small group sessions. These guides are at the end of the text and give directions for six one-hour sessions.

INDIVIDUAL STUDY

You can study this book on your own as well as in a group. Carefully work through each chapter, completing each Personal Learning Activity as it appears in the text. You will be introduced to fresh ideas. Take time to consider and to evaluate each one.

Requirements for receiving credit in the Church Study Course for the study of this book are at the end of the text. (See table of Contents.)

Introduction

"Who are you?" is a game people play. People try to hide who they really are and project an image of something they would like to be. T. S. Eliot calls this universal deception the art of being "hollow men." When asked, Who are you? the usual response is to give one's name. Much can be learned about persons from the way they give their names. Titles often are used to reenforce or bolster a sense of self-importance. Persons who insist on introducing themselves by title such as Doctor, Reverend, Countess, or Madame may be drawing on position to reenforce personhood.

When we get past the name stage of identifying ourselves, we usually go to job descriptions. I am a clerk, an engineer, a consultant. If a person says, I'm just a laborer, or just a housewife, or just a student, we see the reflection of a low self-esteem. We also see the results of a society that has made persons feel that their tasks are unimportant.

After name and job descriptions, the answers branch out to shared relationships. I'm a friend of your uncle's. I know your pastor. I am a father. I am a Baptist. With much probing, we may find out who another person is. Some persons answer directly or indirectly: I'm lonely. I'm hurt. I'm insecure. We pick up these signals more from body language than we do from verbal expression. I was astonished, then gratified, when a man recently responded to my question, "Who are you?" with the candid admission, "I am a cancer patient." I was complimented that he would feel free to tell me first what was currently most important in his self-identity. "Know yourself" was the advice of an ancient Greek philosopher. It is no easy job. It is hard to put people in a book.

PURPOSE

Of the making of books there is no end. The making of books is done by man. And no subject has so intrigued authors as that of their own humanity. This book proposes to express a Christian analysis of mankind. It is a fearsome task.

The question from Psalm 8:4, "What is man . . .?" has received numberless answers. Two brief answers express opposite views. "God created man in his own image" (Gen. 1:27). Man is what he eats (Ludwig Feuerbach). Between these definitions are scores of others, which refine, qualify, and elaborate on various facets and dimensions of personhood.

Whole divisions of natural sciences are given to defining man. Biology and its subdivision sciences study the physical composition of man. Sociology is the science that explores man in his social relationships. Psychology is the science that deals with man's own reflections of himself—his mind and emotions. Theology is the science that speaks of man and his relation to God. This book is a theological book about man.

Every science, unless it remains at the level of pure theory or research, has practical purposes and arts that are used to apply the knowledge gained. One art of biology is medicine. An art of sociology is city planning. An art of psychology is counseling. An art of theology is ministry and churchmanship. *This book is designed to help Christians minister to persons and to help church members make that relation a vital part of understanding themselves and of helping others.*

ORGANIZATION

This book is divided into three parts reflecting an ancient view of personhood: the age of innocence, the age of responsibility, the age of fulfillment.

Part 1: The Age of Innocence *(Chaps. 1–2.)*

In the age of innocence, original man was able not to sin or to die. That idealized condition no longer prevails, but it is necessary to reflect on "the first Adam" in order to speak of the relationships between God and man, time and eternity, history and faith. The first Adam represents a time of ideals and uncluttered possibilities. He is the idealized backdrop on which the darkness of present existence is etched (chap. 1).

Adam the individual is a model of Adam the universal. Man is not fully person in isolation. Personhood is inevitably bound up with other people. Adam the individual is also representative for the race. So is the second Adam, Christ. Western individualism and the fragmentation of modern society lull us into individual selfishness. This selfish individualism is a serious problem for the modern Western world. Persons cannot survive physically, psychologically, or spiritually on a planet where commonality with others is not known (chap. 2).

Part 2: The Age of Responsibility *(Chaps. 3–8.)*
In the age of responsibility man must sin and he must die. It is man's plight to be born to have unhampered fellowship with God yet to be bound to sinfulness and finitude. The reality of existence as we know it gives us much flexibility. There are many activities persons can do. There are many ways to measure man. Man has invented tools and perfected technology. Yet mankind also must have its leisure and its play. Man is a goal-oriented creature. Whether persons know it or not, their ultimate goal is God—their source (chap. 3).

Man, made in the image of God, is responsible for his relationship to God. Without exception, persons have failed to take full responsibility for what they could become. The image of the Father that humanity was meant to bear has been fractured by a fall. Only one son reflects what God is really like. His reflection of the Father and his relation to the Father are unique. Therefore, the Christian community has a special title for Jesus of Nazareth—the Son of God (chap. 4).

Man was made a total being by the creative act of God. Man is wholly soul and body. Since man is made to live in relationship to earth and in relationship to God, he has dual loyalties but only one center. The Greek philosophers divided man. The idealists deny man's kinship to the world. The naturalists deny his relationship to God. Christian Scripture helps persons become the full selves they are intended to be, as individuals and in community (chap. 5).

Yet the responsible self has not acted responsibly. The great wound of man is sin. And the essence of sin is pride, rebellion, greed, and sloth. Sins are acts that grow out of a sinful disposition. A Christian book about man has to deal with the problem of sin (chap. 6). The distinctive and exclusive Christian answer to man's sin problem is God's acceptance (chap. 7). Accepting

God's acceptance is what conversion is all about. To be accepted by God is to live out of a posture of faith and confidence. The gospel is for people. It is basically simple. Some find the good news of God's acceptance too simple. Men inevitably want to do their share. Our share is striving with God's help out of an attitude of faith and awareness of acceptance. No amount of striving will bring salvation. But from a place in the secure knowledge of God's acceptance, we can work toward becoming what we should be. The Christian community has no illusions about how difficult this struggle is. It also has no reservations about God's willingness to help us in the struggle (chap. 8).

Part 3: The Age of Fulfillment *(Chap. 9)*
The third section of the book deals with the age of fulfillment. This age deals with God's ultimate intention and its accomplishment. Through Jesus Christ and the Holy Spirit who indwells his body, the church, God has begun to accomplish his intention for creation (chap. 9). God intends life for his creation. God's purpose involves a kind and quality of life that includes fellowship with God. However, there are the dividers that stand between man and God's ultimate intention. One such divider is death. Death is a temporary divider of man from God; but the threat and anxiety of death casts a foreboding shadow over much of human life. Man himself raises the most abiding and awesome barrier between himself and God. This barrier is rejection, and it creates "the great divorce." The stubborn persistence of God gathers what he has made. His patience and acceptance recreates men. The final destiny of man in Christ is the dynamic place and state of a growing existence before God. We call it heaven.

At the end of the age God will renew his creation. The book of Revelation describes this renewal as the new heaven and earth. Obviously, persons are involved, so is the rest of creation. Jesus is called the firstborn among many brethren (Rom. 8:29). God is concerned for all of his children, and he desires that none should perish. Yet there are those who refuse to believe, even when confronted with the good news of God's acceptance; and they must bear the responsibility for their rejection. Those who reject perceive God's love as wrath. The sorrowful expression of the compassionate Christ, who extended himself to Jerusalem, ends with the solemn declaration, "But ye would not." To those who do receive and fulfill God's intention through Jesus Christ, there is the joy of God's comforting presence and the vision of his person. Redemption is the realization of God's glory and the acknowledgment of our own fulfillment and gratitude for his blessings. To give God glory is also to realize our fullest potential.

Persons move away from God's original intention into the stream of estrangement. By the pressure and power of grace they move, finally, to a condition of fulfillment. A Christian doctrine of man has, indeed, a word about man which is not found in other studies and expressions about the human condition. The special Christian word is that man, the creature of God, is intended for fellowship with the Creator. Man, the total person, may be fully and wholly redeemed because of God's act towards us in Jesus Christ. Man in his social and geographical contexts is responsible for all of his relationships. Ultimate responsibility, like ultimate purpose, comes from beyond our own existence. They come from God, the guarantor of value and the conclusion and goal of existence. It is my hope that this book will help its readers to discover who they are—who they really are in the fullness of their being, in the light of and from the view of the one who gives us our being.

Books are to be read, but having been read, they become one more activity of the past. This is true unless thoughts and experiences in the book become a motivating part of who we are. Even the Bible remains useless to the reader who does not read with understanding and a willingness to learn.

Bring to this study a determination to hear and evaluate a Christian word about persons. Let some of the words of the book find incarnation in actions. Let some of the descriptions become new and exciting ways to express what you feel in your Christian experience and what you hope for in your Christian commitment. It is desirable that a doctrinal expression about man will help you understand the individual who is yourself. From this basis of self-understanding and the awareness of your acceptance by God reach toward other persons. These actions will translate words from pages of a book to lives in our world.

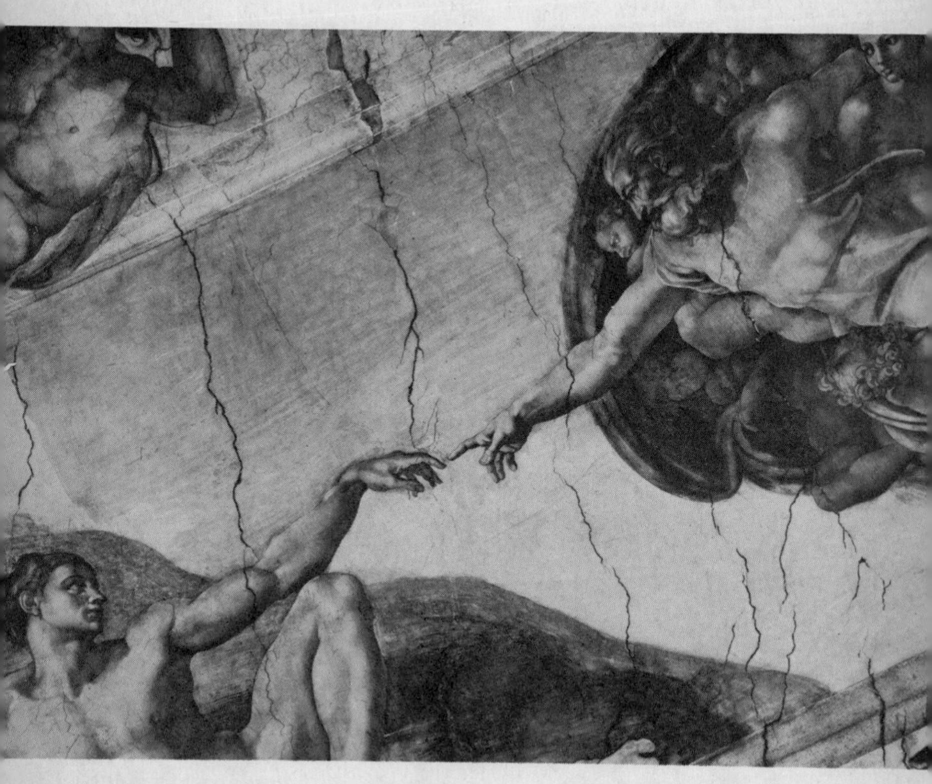

Man was made a total being by the creative act of God. The great lesson Adam teaches us is the fact of our root in God and the necessity of reaching out to one another.

Part 1

The Age of Innocence

Chapter 1
The First Adam

America is considering a move to the metric system. It is traumatic to change a standard that has regulated your life to one with which you are not familiar. From miles to kilometers, from inches to centimeters, from pounds to kilos—it is quite a hassle. All of the same things are going to be measured. It is the scale that is different.

A Christian view of man is a change of standards. Persons are not to be measured by looks or weight or wealth. They are valued from the eye of eternity. An overview of people and their lives from God's dimension provides a different way of measuring the basics of human life. A Christian view of personhood begins in faith and not only in history. The Christian scale weighs people all together, for in this new system of value all people weigh equally and the total weight and worth of people can be determined by the way of the first Adam and the second Adam. This chapter gives the clues for the conversion from measuring persons by a natural system to measuring persons by an ultimate system. It will require some time and patience to catch on to the new system. It always does.

Adam was first, but he really was not first because Christ was first. Christ was prior in time and in preeminence. He shows us who Adam was meant to be and who we are meant to be.

The first man Adam became a living being; the last Adam became a life-giving Spirit (1 Cor. 15:45).

"You go first" is the plea of a child who is nervous about a new experience. "Somebody has to be first" is the logical fact used both by timid people who push the job off on others and by creative adventurers who always want to be first. Being first can happen by accident or by achievement. It is not necessarily desirable to be the first person on the scene of an accident. It is far better to place first in the mile run.

The Bible asserts there are two Adams. The one was first because his existence in our time and space came first. The second Adam, Christ, was first in order of accomplishment and excellence. We may learn something about who we are from both. Each is first—but for different reasons. No other person can ever be first as Adam was or as Christ was. No other human can be first in time as Adam was. No person can attain the eternal and qualitative firstness of Jesus Christ. Yet without their firstness we cannot make sense of our troubled existence or of our possible destiny.

THE RELATION OF TIME AND ETERNITY

There is a tired but amusing comedy routine taken from the world of baseball about who's on first base. The questioner asks, "Who is catcher?" The jokester replies, "No, Who's on first." There is a theological version of the story. The first Adam (Adam) is really the second Adam (because Christ existed in eternity before Adam existed on earth) and the second Adam (Christ) is really the first Adam (since he is the firstborn of all creation [Col. 1:15]).

An elementary truth lies behind this paradox. There are two realms of existence—time and eternity. Christian Scripture and the Christian answer to the riddle of our personhood is deeply rooted in the existence of these two dimensions and the differences between them. For we are, by birth, a part of time; and we are destined, by the intention of God, to participate in eternity.

Time

The idea of time is an involved and complicated study. Is time like a straight line with a beginning, a middle, and an end (as we think in the West)? Or is time a circle that keeps repeating itself (as in Eastern thought)? Is time moving toward a goal (as in Christianity)? Or is time an implacable foe to be escaped (as in Buddhism)? Have men always measured time like we measure time? No, as evidenced by lunar calendars versus solar calendars. Is all time of the same kind? No. Some time is merely chronological. All hours are the same to the clock. But in the consciousness of persons, we speak of time as flying or dragging. An hour of play passes quickly. An hour of waiting for the surgical report of a loved one goes slowly. In the history of nations and in the providence of God, there are special times. The American Revolution was a special time in American history. The biblical expression for special times is "in the fulness of time."

By virtue of birth, persons are bound by time. God has appointed to everything its time and season. In every person's life there are the particular and special times. Man cannot say that individual human existence is good simply because it is lived a long time (Methuselah). Some short lives have accomplished more and have lived more fully (Jesus). Men are responsible for whatever time they have. The Bible speaks of redeeming the time (Eph. 5:16), and the Bible puts an urgent request before us, "Behold, now is the day of salvation" (2 Cor. 6:2). Whatever the relationship of time and eternity, we must acknowledge that what we do in time affects how we possess eternity.

Eternity

The reverse is also true. Eternity molds and shapes our view and use of time. It is difficult to define time. It is even more difficult to define eternity. According to the Christian understanding, time and eternity interact. Time came into being when the eternal God created it. Time will cease to exist when the eternal God consummates it. Life in time is enlightened when the Son of God breaks into it. Eternity is different from what it would have been had Jesus Christ not brought his human dimension of historical experience into the eternal order.

We cheapen eternity if we reduce it to nothing more than endless time. Duration is a quality of eternity, but it is not the distinctive quality. Endless time filled with boredom or unbearable pain is not a happy prospect. Eternity is a meaningful type of being that fulfills existence. We now live surrounded by eternity. And eternity, having broken into our time, brings it added meaning. A beautiful and poetic way of saying this is, "He hath written eternity in our hearts" (see Eccl. 3:11).

Eternity is God's time. This means that he is not bound by our finitude. He does not live under our conditions. Therefore, there is the possibility of outside help for us. Our understanding of who we are does not have to be bound to time. This is an important clue to the question of who we are. In establishing human identity, eternity, as well as time, must be considered.

True humanity has more to do with the second Adam, Christ, than with the first Adam. Believing is a key to existing.

PERSONAL LEARNING ACTIVITY 1
The writer has said that "eternity molds and shapes our view and use of time." How have your values and actions been influenced by the Christian view that time is a part of eternity and is moving toward a goal of eternal significance? Write a brief paragraph stating your answer to this question. Then give three examples of persons whose values and use of time were changed by the Christian concept of the relation of time and eternity.

THE RELATION OF FAITH AND HISTORY

The next clue to a discovery of a Christian understanding of man has to do with faith and history. Faith is a special way of looking at life, and history is a special way of recording what seems important in life. A Christian understanding of persons must ask what people believe and how and why they record what seems important.

The Bible, which provides the indispensable clues for a Christian understanding of man, is a book of faith. "Now faith is the assurance of things hoped for, the conviction of things not seen" (Heb. 11:1, RSV). Faith is not the opposite of reason. It is a bias—a special way of reasoning. The reasoning of faith grows out of one radical commitment which shapes all our thought.

People share many common biases. For example, persons are better than animals. Persons are superior in ability to plants. My senses will report correctly what I see, touch, taste, smell, or feel. Most people have faith in themselves. Most people have faith in, a bias toward, those they love. Many people have faith in the government and in the news media. Personal and social crises come when one no longer has faith in himself, the ones he loves, the government, the media. The bias of faith may change to disillusionment and disappointment. And with that change there is a loss of self-identity. Who is to be believed? Who is to be trusted?

I once worked at a children's home where there were many crises of identity. Many of the children and young adults in that home lost faith in themselves, and in practically everything else, when their parents proved unworthy of their faith and favorable bias or trust. It is also a normal process of adolescence to lose the absolute faith young children place in their parents. Much of the human quest is a search for someone or something to have absolute faith in. Man's life is a contradiction. On the one hand, he must live out of faith. On the other hand, he finds many objects of his faith unworthy of his confidence and trust.

A clue to a Christian understanding of man found in the Bible is the clue of faith. Since people live out of faith, to be fulfilled they must have faith in (a bias toward) something that is secure and eternal. This is why I stated that history is enlightened and informed by eternity. The Christian affirmation is that God the Father as revealed in Jesus the Son and as witnessed to by the Holy Spirit is the adequate object of faith.

The Bible is a book of faith. What is recorded in the Bible was considered important by its authors. Their one radical faith commitment was that God was the sole basis for faith. Therefore, they saw history in the light of their faith. The Christian community has shared the biblical writers' faith commitment that God is the adequate object of faith. Christians also affirm that what the biblical authors said about God and man is true. The Christian community is delightfully biased toward the Bible and toward its message. In the Bible, faith is a way of looking at reality; and history is the selection of the realities at which faith looks. The objective facts and occurrences in time were seen differently by other faith viewpoints. For example, the court records of Cyrus the Persian would not reflect that he was God's instrument of judgment. The Roman procurator Pontius Pilate did not share the early Christian view that Jesus was the Savior of the world. The Bible reflects a certain interpretation of events. The Christian community believes that this interpretation is true to God's intention. The Bible is a book of faith and a book of history. History cannot prove faith, for faith is the selecting force that gives rise to every history. To suppose that history is an objective science that can judge the Bible or confirm it is false. The historian who seeks either to prove or to disprove the Bible is already working out of a certain faith bias.

Our search for self-identity has provided two clues. We are not bound purely by time in assessing what persons are. Persons should be seen also in the light of eternity, God's time. Second, persons live from faith. A Christian feels that the basic faith commitment is to God himself. Christians also believe that what God desires for and thinks about persons is recorded in the Bible. They further believe that the Bible is a book of faith that has selected important events to express a right perspective about God and man.

THE RELATION OF ADAM TO ALL MEN

One thing the Bible suggests about persons is that they are all bound together. Each man is connected to every other man. The event of Adam is important to insure the solidarity of the race. The theological affirmation that people are inevitably related is even more significant than tracing a first couple to a geographical area. They are related because God is the creator of all that exists. They are related because they are alike biologically and psychologically. However numerous the distinctions among individuals, their similarity is more significant. Without a common bone structure the art of orthopedic surgery would not be possible. Without a universal need for recognition and acceptance the psychological and social sciences would not exist. Without all persons' need for the God who gives them being religion would be meaningless. All branches of sciences and the arts that are drawn from them suppose that people have something in common. The great lesson Adam teaches us is the fact of our root in God and the necessity of reaching out to one another.

In the account of the first man's creation in Genesis 1 there is a further clue about personhood. People are different from all other created things. Genesis 1 puts this difference in terms of man's dominance over creation. The crown of creation is man and woman. "Male and female created he them" (Gen. 1:27). The dominion of people often has been a curse to animals and the world of nature. The dominion of which the Bible speaks is not an irresponsible type of priority. The implication is plain. People are responsible for the planet. They hold their responsibility before God. Later in the book we will spell out the responsibility. In this chapter our clue is the distinction of persons. People are assessed from God's dimension in the light of fullest personhood—in Christ. People receive their distinction from the hand of God, and the stewardship of dominion is a particularly human responsibility.

Genesis 2 provides two additional clues in our search for a theological meaning of personhood. Man is formed from the substance of earth, and he is infused with the substance of heaven. The biological and geological sciences assert and describe man's relation to earth. Biblical revelation explains man's unwillingness to be content ultimately with only the things of earth. A beautiful, poetic description of man's more than earthliness is found in the Apocrypha.

> The Lord created man out of earth,
> and turned him back to it again.
> He gave to men few days, a limited time,
> but granted them authority over the things upon the earth.
> He endowed them with strength like his own,
> and made them in his own image.
> He placed the fear of them in all living beings,
> and granted them dominion over beasts and birds.
> He made for them tongue and eyes;
> he gave them ears and a mind for thinking.
> He filled them with knowledge and understanding,
> and showed them good and evil.
> He set his eye upon their hearts
> to show them the majesty of his works.
> And he gave them to boast of his marvels for ever.
>
> (*Ecclesiasticus 17:1–9,* RSV)

Man's kinship with earth should make him sympathetic in his stewardship of dominion over his context. Man's legacy from heaven makes him aware of the dignity of all persons. A recent book speaks of a human engineering of people which must be accomplished at the expense of freedom and dignity.[1] Our dignity is a happy remnant of our legacy from Adam, and biblical faith cannot approve any engineering that violates that dignity.

Genesis 2 also speaks of man's need for community. The first man found no companion in any creation of God. The gracious act of creating woman as counterpart to man is a way of stressing man's completion only in social relationship with persons. The first and obvious filling of the need for community is at the level of man-woman correspondence. The biological possibility for the continuance of the human race lies in the fact of human sexuality—male and female. The possibility for the psychological health of humanity rests in right social relationships with others. The theological possibility of becoming a whole person with full dignity lies in an individual relationship to the corporate body of Christ. At every level, the individual needs community.

Primitive societies know the power and punishment of isolation. Ostracism from friends and family can bring psychological and even physical death. Spiritual death lurks in the final loneliness of being cut off from God and from other persons. People are created to relate to the world and womb which nourished them. Man in isolation is less than human. He who is made for God bears the lingering life of God's breath. Our continued and corporate existence finally is lost when we do not continue to breathe God's breath and when we do not touch the living life of God in others.

Adam and Eve are the necessary first occurrences and typical figures of these truths. As parents of "all living," they are the original patterns of all who have lived. From the distinctiveness of this first couple we move to the universal and general. Mankind is responsible for the world. Persons are chemical in composition and are granted their ultimate worth and dignity by the breath of God. Human companionship is a requirement for fulfilled humanity.

PERSONAL LEARNING ACTIVITY 2
The preceding divisions of this chapter suggest four clues that help us gain a Christian understanding of man. Review this part of the chapter and underscore each clue.

INNOCENCE VERSUS PERFECTION

The first Adam indicates a special condition of existence. He was innocent. At that time the question was whether to sin or not to sin. But it is no longer the question today. Our dilemma is what to do with the inevitability of our sinfulness. Innocence is not perfection. Perfection comes by testing and overcoming. Perfection is the province of the second Adam. Perfection is to be associated, as we shall see, with the Garden of Paradise. Innocence is the hallmark of Eden.

In order to speak of a fall, we must assume a higher state. One way we can express our deficiencies is in the light of a prior "golden age." An age of innocence is found in the teachings of most primitive religions. The desire to return to the innocence of our childhood and the childhood of the race is one of the most pathetic desires men have. It is pathetic because it is impossible. Yet, the possibility provides the backdrop against which we play out the drama of our guilt and responsibility.

The contrast of innocence and perfection highlights the difference between the first Adam and the second. The first Adam speaks of the innocence that might have been. The second Adam speaks of the perfection that is to come. The biblical message and all human history is bracketed on one hand by the innocence of unfallen Adam and the perfection of the resurrected Christ. It is between these brackets, at the borders of history and eternity, that we live.

SUMMARY

A theological view of personhood tells us things about ourselves that other sources cannot. (1) Man is measured in the light of eternity as well as time. (2) The Bible tells of man's beginning from a faith perspective. (3) Christ as second Adam explains what man should be. Clues for genuine humanity are found in him who was first both in point of time and in point of excellence. (4) Mankind, for all its distinctions and individualities, is one. The species that categorizes us (humanity) is stronger than that which separates us (our individual differences). (5) Man's responsibility for the world is a gift of God that may be used well or badly. (6) Man's dual nature relates him to both earth and heaven. Therefore, man never can be content merely to be like all of the other creatures. (7) Man is a social being. Isolation is not God's intention for people. (8) First Adam represents innocence; the last Adam embodies perfection. All people in between are neither of these. We are on the road between them. How we got there and the difficulty of the dilemma of living between the brackets of innocence and perfection is a story that will be told in the remainder of the book.

PERSONAL LEARNING ACTIVITY 3

Consider each of the preceding summary statements. What is one thing that each helps you understand about yourself?

NOTE

1. B. F. Skinner, *Beyond Freedom and Dignity* (New York: Alfred A. Knopf, Inc., 1971).

Chapter 2

The One and the Many

A primary principle in criminology is to look for a pattern in recurring crimes. Certain notorious criminals have captured public fancy by leaving a definite and discernible trace at the scene of the crime. All people bear the marks of both a good Creator and a cosmic criminal. Everyone has something in common with everyone else, for God made all of us. An old classic motto puts it this way: "I am human; therefore anything that concerns humanity is of concern to me." Of all of God's creatures, man was intended to be the highest. But there is also a pattern of distortion that occurs in each of us. The demonic has left a trace upon us as well. So has the divine.

The rabbis tell the story that when God created Adam, he took dust from the four corners of the earth. The ancient Persians speak of Goyamart, the first man. He was created bright and white eyed and all human life came from him.[1]

Greek mythology speaks of the creation of mankind from the elements of earth, air, fire, and water.[2] Persons are one with the earth and are invested with a soul placed into their body.

An old Latin quotation says, "I am a man; therefore, I cannot be unconcerned with what happens to all men."

Every culture and religious community seeks for and asserts belief in a commonness of all persons. The biblical way of expressing the solidarity of all people is to speak of our first parents and to declare that all persons come from a common stock. In chapter 1 we explored the relation of the first Adam and Christ, the second Adam. We also saw the necessity of relating all persons to one another. This chapter continues the study of man's age of innocence by noting how man is related to all creation by virtue of our common Creator. All that exists is bound in bonds of dependence on God and on other created things. Only persons can, by their rebellion, seek independence from God and other created beings. In this arrogant striving for total independence from God, we see the fall. The fall represents the transition from innocence to responsibility. Even in fallenness, persons share a common fate. Mankind expresses its solidarity even in its sinfulness. However, the sin of Adam does not produce our guilt. The first transgression sets the inevitable tempo of man's continuing journey in sin. But Adam does not make us do it.

This important chapter deals with (1) the interrelatedness of persons with all creation, (2) all persons' universal and inevitable sinfulness before God, and (3) the effect of the fall on all persons.

CREATION FROM A COMMON HAND

"In the beginning God created the heaven and the earth." This simple, profound declaration contains two ideas essential to Christian faith. God existed first. Elemental logic demands that God was there; else how could he create? All that exists had its being because God created, willed, or permitted it. This absolute affirmation means that creation comes from a common hand.

The declaration "and God saw that it was good" is sprinkled throughout the account of creation in Genesis 1. All that God created was good. Even though this is no longer true of all things, Christians cannot forget God's original pronouncement and affirmation. We must not forget that creation was good, for this declares God's intention for what he had made. The world was good, man was good, the plants that grow, all things that were were good. These descriptions of original creation also apply to redeemed creation. Therefore, the Christian community that knows how things were and how they are going to be must declare the goodness of God's work despite all evidence to the contrary.

This is our Father's world. God is good, and he declared what he made to be good. One small girl captured this message when she said: "I must be okay, because God made me. And God don't make no junk." Creation comes from a common hand, and it is the good hand of God. Later, this chapter speaks of how God's good creation becomes evil. But we dare not glorify evil to such an extent that we permit it to shut out the way things were and the way they were meant to be.

God was first. All else that is is because he created or permits it. The age of innocence reminds us that God's creation was good. The fact that creation comes from a common hand means also that all that has creaturely existence is dependent.

CREATED ORDERS—DEPENDENT AND INDEPENDENT

There is a special word that means the dependence of one life on other lives. The word is *symbiosis.* Symbiosis should become a very big part of Christians' vocabularies. Surely Christians should know better than others that all life is dependent on God, the ground of life.

But a person's life is also dependent on other forms of life and on the lives of others. The biblical account of creation expresses that God gave vegetation to sustain man and the beasts (Gen. 1:29). Possibly the omission of meat occurs in order to sustain the symbolism that until the sin of persons there is no shedding of the blood of beasts. What is involved is a reverence for life as well as a provision for life.

The orders of creation imply a hierarchy of value. Vegetation is given to sustain the other forms of life. Animals are given to describe the variety and fullness of creation. (It should be remembered that Genesis describes all that is, as well as asserting who made it. And a description of the natural world which omits animal life would be incomplete indeed.) Later in the Bible animals will be acknowledged as food for man, as beasts of burden to serve man, and as substitutionary sacrifices for the sin of man. Mankind is viewed as the crown of the created order. But our predisposition to think of ourselves in isolation and as independent from the rest of creation has lead us to overlook how dependent we are on other created substances for our existence.

The ancient Greeks spoke of four basic substances—earth, air, fire, and water. Modern chemistry has isolated several dozen elements. One thing is certain. All created substances and the elements of which they are composed interact. We could not live if oxygen were not present. Animals could not exist without water. Plants could not grow without light. Ours is indeed a world that is wondrously made. And a large part of the wonder is that it fits together so well. God made all things good. He also made all things dependent on him and on other things.

Truth and reality have two sides. Creation is dependent, but it is also independent. Every general group is composed of individuals. The independence of individuality is good, but it also carries the possibility of evil. When the independence of the individual becomes an arrogant independence from God and from and over other people and things, there is trouble in Eden.

"HE SAW US RUINED IN THE FALL"

The sad sequel to Genesis 1—2 is Genesis 3. Genesis 3 is the recurring script in the life of every person. Innocence is the golden period when things were as they were supposed to be. Eden is the childhood of the race. And in the midst of the Garden is the tree of the knowledge of good and evil. It is forbidden. As long as man is innocent, he cannot be responsible. How easy is the childhood in which all needs are provided. Eden is where "every prospect pleases." Milton said of it:

> . . . a circling row
> Of goodliest trees laden with fairest fruit,
> Blossoms and fruits at once of golden hue
> Appeared, with gay enameled colors mixed:
> On which the sun more glad impressed his beams
> Than in fair evening cloud, or humid bow,
> When God hath showered the earth; so lovely seemed
> That landscape: . . .
>
> John Milton, *Paradise Lost,* Book IV, lines 146–153

But in the midst of innocence, there is the possibility of resistance. In the delights of dependence, there is the chance of an independence that wants to be as God. There is an outside occasion, the serpent, that drives and seduces to internal rebellion. This rebellion, an intense act of the will, becomes sin, an external act committed by our total selves. There was a first such act, and all persons invariably repeat it. This act of arrogant independence we call the fall. The essence and nature of sin will be discussed later. What must be said now is that the goodness of creation is clouded by the reality of sin. When man seeks an arrogant independence from God, the consequences are far-reaching. There are ruptured relationships. Fallen man hides from the presence of God. Fallen persons blame one another for their own acts of rebellious independence. Fallen people cannot live in Eden.

Since all creation is interrelated, the Bible suggests that all creation suffers because of man's sin. This is not mere poetic expression. Animals suffer the cruelty of warped persons. The land is violated by those who use it selfishly. Paul's expression is that "the whole creation has been groaning in travail" (Rom. 8:22, RSV). The familiar Christmas hymn puts it poetically: "No more let sins and sorrows grow, Nor thorns infest the ground; He comes to make his blessings flow far as the curse is found." God's declaration to Adam " 'Cursed is the ground because of you' " (Gen. 3:17, RSV) has a far-reaching consequence.

One consequence of sin is the alienation of persons from God. "He saw me ruined in the fall" is a powerful expression from the old hymn "Awake, My Soul, in Joyful Lays." Another consequence of the fall is alienation from others. Adam's excuse "The woman whom thou gavest to be with me" (Gen. 3:12) is glaring evidence that self-justification is the most harmful of all sins. A third consequence of sin is the alienation from one's context. The sinner is expelled from the innocence of Eden into a hostile world. Honest labor is not a curse, but the toil and anxiety that accompany it are.

Why should there be, why must there be a fall? Philosophers and theologians have written endlessly on that perennial question. The Bible, a thoroughly realistic book, does not ask or answer the question. It picks up with the consequences and begins the record of the long task of undoing what sin has done.

A case can be made for the idea that the fall was an upward fall which brought man independence and responsibility. No fall, no redemption. But ultimately the aspect of disaster must be stressed. The fall is not essentially good. Evil has corrupted good. Man's individuality has become a prison for his isolation. Our freedom has produced evil which causes both us and God to suffer. There is no point in asking if it might not be better if we remain in Eden. That is not our option. The step from innocence to responsibility involves both man and God. We have not carried the weight of our responsibility well. But God has remained true to his responsibility for creation. And it is because of God's fidelity to his responsibility that Christians can speak of "the assurance of things hoped for, the conviction of things not seen" (Heb. 11:1, RSV).

The transition from innocence to responsibility is complete. No one can return again to the womb, and no one can return to the innocence of Eden. But we are not left alone in our responsibility. God's mercy is shown even in man's being cast out of Eden. If Adam had eaten of the tree of life, the second tree in the Garden, he would have lived forever in his state of rebellion. He was excluded so that he could not obtain an earthly immortality in sin. It was a gracious act of God, who still intends and will bring to pass his intention that his creation shall be good. A second line must be added to the phrase from the hymn quoted previously. "He saw me ruined in the fall, Yet loved me notwithstanding all."

A final consequence of sin is death. A man's most independent and individual act is his death. The fall leaves its question of finitude. Is death the end? Is good really gone? Our only hope is a death of death. Since mankind was excluded from the tree of life in Eden, it is appropriate that God shall renew this fruit in the tree of life which stands in the garden of God at the end of time. This is, of course, seeing the end of the story from the beginning. And we must not rush God's timetable. We live between the innocence of Eden and the fulfillment of the coming age. Ours is the time of full responsibility. But questions arise about our responsibility.

PERSONAL LEARNING ACTIVITY 4
For this activity, use the most recent issue of your newspaper available. Rewrite each headline on the front page to read as you think it would if all persons still lived in a state of innocence. Then contemplate the contrasts and meditate on the full meaning of the fall.

ADAM DIDN'T MAKE ME DO IT

A well-known television comedian has made popular the statement, "The Devil made me do it!" The statement always gets laughs. In reality, it is no laughing matter. The full Christian doctrine of man will assert both that man is responsible for his own sin and that there are powerful extenuating circumstances that make necessary the sinfulness of all persons.

A misunderstanding of the doctrine of original sin has been

used to deny individual responsibility for sin. This doctrine is based on Romans 5:12–21 and 1 Corinthians 15:20–28. There have been much ink and tears shed over interpretations of these passages. A popular misconception of the doctrine is as follows. When Adam fell in the Garden, he became a sinner; and every one of his descendants inherits that sin from him. Therefore, everyone who is born has this spiritual taint, gained by being conceived and being born. All who are born are sinners. Sinners who do not repent go to hell. Therefore, anyone who dies before repenting goes to hell. Since we are sinners by birth, we had no choice in the matter. Therefore, Adam is responsible, and God seems unfair.

This, in its boldest expression, is a popular understanding of original sin. If this is the truth of the matter, it is small wonder that some Christian communities seek to put infants under the protection of God by some ordinance such as baptism. But, in my opinion, the popular understanding of original sin expressed here is based on a wrong interpretation of Romans 5 and 1 Corinthians 15. Paul does assert a relationship between Adam and all men. He sees Adam as a type and representative of what all men are and do. Note carefully Romans 5:12. This verse says death came into the world through one man, but it spread "because all men sinned" (RSV). First Corinthians 15:21 is talking about resurrection. The verse seeks to establish that death is universal and it came about first in Adam. Then resurrection also is universal because it came about in Christ. Paul gives no statement about sin being transmitted automatically or physically from parent to child. The fact that there was a first occurrence is followed by the affirmation that all have sinned. First Corinthians 15 cannot be made to say that all are condemned because of what Adam did unless one is also willing to say that all men are saved because of what Christ did. If sin is automatic, so is salvation.

THEN WHY DO PEOPLE SIN?

It is appropriate to speak of all persons as sinful. It is correct to say they become sinners when they actualize their sinful inclination. Evil does have an edge. All persons inevitably seek their way above God's way. But no person is condemned until he does exercise his own radical individuality in such a way as to be destructive to himself and to break the relationship with God. Parents need not mourn the destiny of a child who dies in infancy. The child is with God. God who made all things good is the strong defender of the weak, the helpless, the unresponsible.

Why all persons sin is a difficult problem. There is no completely satisfactory answer. However, several theories have been suggested. One theory is that the answer can be stated in terms of *freedom.* There must be the act of evil before good assumes full meaning. Another theory is that the answer can be stated in terms of *divine intention.* God purposed that redemption would bring blessings in fulfillment that are not possible for innocence. The fall is the inevitable prelude to the cross. A third theory is that the answer can be stated in terms of *mystery.* It is unfathomable why God permitted evil. Classical theologians spoke of this as the "mystery of iniquity."

It is best to acknowledge that theories of why people sin do not answer the pressing question of what you do with a real condition. The human condition is this. All persons come to states of selfishness and unfulfillment that limit their existence. In those states of rebellious pride and in the acts that come from them we deny the Creator's intention for us. Paul calls this coming short of the glory of God. The condition is inevitable, but it is not irreversible. The possibility of reversing our estrangement from God is the promise of the gospel. Our estrangement from the perfect good that God intends for us is the result of our own attitudes and actions. Adam did not make me do it, but I have joined him and all others in the decision to assert my individuality in destructive ways. This is the path of disobedience. It leads to death. What we must do is make another decision in favor of life. That is the decision God enables us to make. In both decisions we have a responsible part.

PERSONAL LEARNING ACTIVITY 5

Write your own paraphrase of either Romans 5:12–21 or 1 Corinthians 15:20–28. This paraphrase should express clearly what you feel to be the meaning of the verses.

NOTES

1. R. C. Zaehner, *The Teaching of the Magi* (New York: Oxford University Press, 1976), p. 74.
2. Plato, *Timaeus,* trans. Benjamin Jowett (New York: Liberal Arts Press, 1949), p. 42.

The biblical message and all human history is bracketed on one hand by the innocence in which man was created and on the other by the perfection of the resurrected Christ. It is between these brackets, at the borders of history and eternity, that we live.

Part 2

The Age of Responsibility

Chapter 3

The Measure of Man

Gourmet cooks have their secrets. Never ask a professional chef to share all the tricks of the trade. These secrets are what give originality and enhance professional skills. Dinner guests often ask a hostess, "What is in this casserole?" They are not inquiring about the obvious ingredients. They are asking about the special savor. People are made up of chemicals and physical properties even as is the rest of creation. There is, however, a special savor to being human. What are the ingredients that make people different from the rest of God's creation?

It is futile to desire to return to the womb of innocence. Man in sin has come of age, and in our maturity we must assess ourselves for what we are. It is a checkered picture. We are both achievers and destroyers. The accomplishments of mankind cannot be overlooked. It ill becomes religion to sneer at the technological achievements of the sciences while enjoying the products of their genius. All created things are neutral until used by persons for good or evil. Likewise, those things man has fabricated and produced can be used either for good or ill. An example of this is synthetic drugs.

To despise our humanity and to treat our bodies as shameful or unworthy is to cast aspersions on both the wisdom of God, the Creator, and the goodness of the humanity of Jesus, the Redeemer.

To make man the measure of all things is to overlook his finitude (he must die) and his perennial problems (he is sinner). Those same civilizations that have reached the heights of accomplishment have destroyed others to achieve their own best ends. Individuals who have contributed to our store of knowledge have been intensely aware of man's failure.

The scientists who produced the atom bomb plead for religious and social values to rise and meet the frightening challenge of the destructive force they had created. The story of Dr. Jekyl and Mr. Hyde is intriguing, for each of us recognizes something of this drama of divisiveness in his own life.

PERSONAL LEARNING ACTIVITY 6
Paul's classic description of the divided self is in Romans 7—8. Read these chapters and list the points of frustration and inner striving Paul experienced. Study your list. How many of these points of frustration and inner striving have you also experienced?

This chapter will point to the positive achievements and abilities of persons. Humanity may be defined and described in a variety of ways. We will look for those things that make persons distinctive and make the life of man enjoyable. It is sobering to realize that personhood may be enjoyed most by those who merely possess it without trying to describe it. Consider the joys of childhood and the relaxed naturalness of people at play.

I am convinced that the serious quest of who we are also can contribute to the important answer of who we ought to be. Four old and recognized functions are used to describe people. Two of the activities of persons which animals also share are the task of work and the art of play. Two capacities that are apparently distinctive to the human species are the ability to think and the possibility of responding to God. In the following divisions of the chapter, I will use four Latin terms to express these time-honored ideas of personhood. I will use *man the worker* to include all of man's technological accomplishments. All the creative and leisure arts will be included under *man the player. Man the thinker* will include all the branches and divisions of man's reflective arts. All ability to respond to God and all religious responses will be considered under *religious man.*

It is well to begin with the positive assessment of man. The Bible stresses that man was created good and that his recreation in Christ is intended to secure his goodness.

MAN THE WORKER

Solomon advised, "Go to the ant, thou sluggard" (Prov. 6:6). It was an attempt to encourage the lazy to be motivated by the industry of insects. Some persons may be lazy, but humankind, as a whole, has shown much desire to work. Whereas animal industry is apparently the result of an instinct, human labor has a creative flair.

Modern man has been especially obedient to the divine injunction to subdue the earth. By clever inventions and mass production we have made possible the good life from the viewpoint of creature comforts. Christians in the developed nations have shared in these comforts. Our dilemmas have arisen not because of our abundance but because of the desperate needs of many persons around the world. Christians need not apologize for contributing to technology and industry. But they should act as sensitive consciences to our society to share with the world the fruits of man's creativity.

Christians face a second dilemma in a technological society where things are in abundance. It is the satisfaction with and the craving for possessions. Perhaps we should print at the top of our charge cards "A man's life does not consist in the abundance of the things he possesses." Having is no substitute for doing. A third dilemma has arisen because there is so much to have and, thanks to laborsaving devices, so little to do. The answer for unemployment has not been found. Formerly, farming machines and assembly lines replaced agricultural laborers and blue collar workers. Now office and business machines are replacing white collar workers. It is humiliating for humans to be replaced by machines. Christian communities also must speak a word for human dignity and provide a context where people can do things machines cannot.

Despite these dilemmas, human creativity is a gift from God. It is mind boggling to realize that within one year's time scientists have discovered that big galaxies eat (absorb) little ones; that there is no life on Mars; and that obesity can be controlled by surgically reducing the size of the stomach.[1]

Perceptive Christians who hear that galaxy 3C123 is eight billion light-years from earth will have an expanded appreciation for Psalm 8:

> O Lord, our Lord, how majestic is thy name in all the earth! Thou whose glory above the heavens is chanted by the mouth of babes and infants, thou hast founded a bulwark because of thy foes, to still the enemy and the avenger. When I look at thy

> heavens, the work of thy fingers, the moon and the stars which thou hast established; what is man that thou art mindful of him, and the son of man that thou dost care for him? Yet thou hast made him little less than God, and dost crown him with glory and honor. Thou hast given him dominion over the works of thy hands; thou hast put all things under his feet, all sheep and oxen, and also the beasts of the field, the birds of the air, and the fish of the sea, whatever passes along the paths of the sea. O Lord, our Lord, how majestic is thy name in all the earth! (RSV).

Modern Christians will understand that our own day is having a firsthand look at the things that pass "along the paths of the sea." This is illustrated by the American submarine expedition that collected samples from an ocean floor six thousand feet below sea level.

The unity of man spoken of in chapter 2 is helping modern medicine profit from antique specimens and techniques. Scientists dealing with respiratory devices are being helped by autopsies performed on mummies. And the ancient oriental technique of acupuncture is being performed now by painless laser beams. When God breathed into man the breath of life, he began something good. Christians must believe this and rejoice in every beneficial accomplishment of man the worker, who now makes tools so sophisticated that even his accomplishments of a decade ago seem outmoded. The Christian gift that accompanies man's progress is hope in the God of the future who lies beyond all progress—the God who grants all progress.

PERSONAL LEARNING ACTIVITY 7
What have you achieved through human labor that has caused you to feel more fulfilled as a person? What part did God play in that achievement?

MAN THE PLAYER

"All work and no play makes Jack a dull boy." When people lived in nomadic, shepherding communities, the pace of life was leisurely and the provisions for life were scarce. They engaged in much physical activity and ate little. Social interchange happened when groups or tribes came together. They practiced the ritualism of stories from the past and exchanged news about the present. All play and leisure were done in the family or at these social conclaves. All entertainment was homegrown.

Work and play are alternated with the planting, tending, and harvesting of crops in agricultural civilizations. Natural forces and natural resources set the schedule. Some seasons were all work and no play and "Jack was indeed a dull boy." In other seasons there was no work, but there was also little incentive to play because of anxiety about food and provisions for existence. Ordinarily the rhythm of nature permitted an alternation between work and play.[2]

Israel's three major religious festivals were centered around both an agricultural calendar and events of God's saving history. As D. B. J. Campbell has noted:

> The earliest Decalogue of the Pentateuch . . . required Hebrew males to observe three festivals. "Three times in the year shall all your males appear before the Lord God, the God of Israel" (Exodus 34:23). So too did the Book of the Covenant, . . . (Exodus 23:14–17). They were the pastoral and agricultural festivals of Passover and Unleavened Bread; the feast of Weeks or First Fruits, better known as Pentecost; the feast of Ingathering or Tabernacles (Exodus 34:18–26).
>
> Other festivals were added later, but the original three reflect the early life of the Hebrew community. Agricultural peoples, the world over, have seen special religious significance in the corn harvest, especially in the first gathered and the last sheaf. Their ancient observances still survive in many local customs.[3]

The alternating rhythm of stress/relax is formed by divine example in the account of creation. God rests on the sabbath. The most essential and elemental lesson to be learned from the sabbath principle is the necessity for time away from the ordinary. To be fully and adequately whole persons we must have some recourse from the ordinary to the diverse. Man is made for play as well as for work. The festivals and prescribed rites of Israel provided for moments of anticipation and joy when "the tribes go up." Interestingly enough, worship and the service of God were regarded as play in the sense of a welcome alternative to the established routine of work.

In a modern technological society, we are faced with the

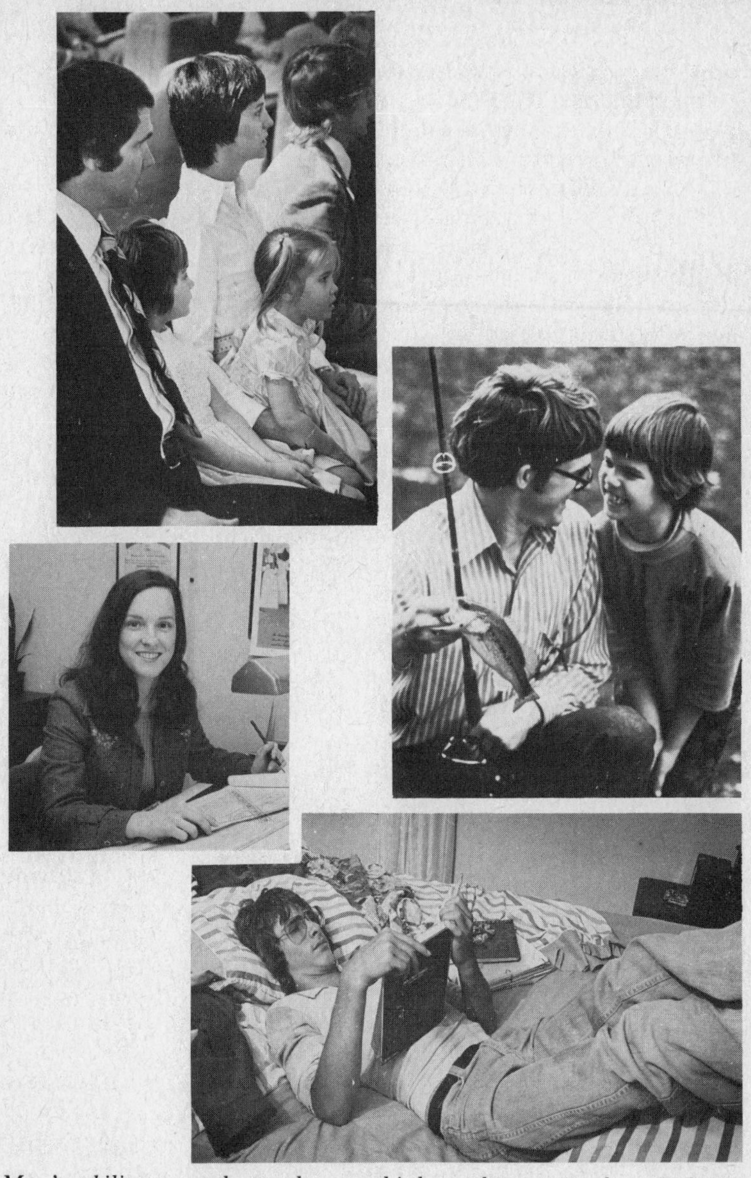

Man's ability to work, to play, to think, and to respond to God are necessary but different parts of his personhood.

opposite problems from those of biblical times or of underdeveloped nations. In an age in which machines can and do replace persons in manual and even in technical skills, there is often too much time for leisure. Families facing a spiraling economy often have many jobs and find their homes serving less and less as a center for family teaching or relaxation. The single largest killer in American society is stress diseases. It seems we are doing more and enjoying it less. We work too hard at play. We have equated fun and play with spectator sports. The new heroes of our time are super athletes whom we dehumanize by selling or trading for excessive amounts of money. Millions of dollars are spent for professional entertainment and for expensive recreational equipment. Nevertheless, one of the greatest detriments to human achievement in our time is boredom.

We often are depriving children of play time by forcing complicated schedules of learning required by modern technology. There is no making up for the lost play of childhood, regardless of how hard we pursue it in middle age. At the other end of existence, we often are cutting off older persons from their fruitful creative work by forcing them into early retirement and leisure. It is ironic that in our culture we force the children who know so well how to play into the serious work of learning, and we force some able older adults who know so well how to work into a life of leisure when they have forgotten how to play.[4]

Christian community must address itself seriously to the fact that man is a player. We must be convinced that the natural rhythm of life, given by God our creator, is strive/relax, create/worship, work/rest. It is not possible for most of us to return to nomadic or agricultural kinds of society. We can be enviously sympathetic with those serious experiments in our time that are striving for a simpler life-style; for example, farm communities in Israel and the return of many young Americans to agricultural areas. However, it is inconceivable that all persons in our society could or would live that way. At the same time we must ask ourselves if too much unstructured time and too many diverse possibilities and activities are contributing to our unhappiness. Religious workers particularly are notorious overachievers who must be convinced at a serious theological level that play and leisure are activities as acceptable to God as meeting and planning are.[5]

Too often worship is work and not play. It is a complicating requirement and not a happy experience that we enjoy. Both the church that conducts worship and the individual who worships have responsibility in planning and participating in worship that is exciting and joyful. All work and no play in the life of a church makes dull Christians.

I have one positive suggestion as to how Christians in our complex society can best become more fully human by their capacity for play. When choosing a job, be sure it is something you enjoy doing. All jobs have their unpleasant moments; but if your life's vocation is filled only with unpleasantness, change jobs. Leisure is not a biblical word. God's work is his play. God both enjoys and is willing to do what he does. Even the necessary and unpleasant prospect of the cross was faced willingly and with the deepest kind of joy that comes from filling one's own destiny.[6]

When our work can be approached in a leisurely and enjoyable manner, our play also will be more creative. To feel that we are forced to work at jobs we hate and then to find we are obliged to have a good time by being entertained is an unfortunate outlook on both work and play. Man is a worker and man is a player. God acknowledges and endorses the rhythm of life that accents both the work of creation and the sabbath rest—both work and play. There remains for our discussion those two positive abilities of man, which only man can perform, thinking and worshiping.

PERSONAL LEARNING ACTIVITY 8
Honestly evaluate the quality of play in your life. List (1) three things you can do to strengthen in your life the rhythm of stress/relax, work/play; (2) three things you can do to make your work a greater source of joy; and (3) three things you can do to find more joy and excitement in your experiences of worship.

MAN THE THINKER

In counting our positive assets, we must reflect on our ability to reason. The ancient Greeks thought the mind to be separate from the body. However, modern people know that mind and body are inevitably interwoven. The Bible teaches that our minds and our bodies are integral parts of a whole person. In the Bible there is the awareness of our inner and outer expressions of our whole being, but these are not understood as parts. So close is the connection of body and thought that human thought is regarded as arising from physical portions of the body. As a man "thinketh in his heart, so is he" (Prov. 23:7). In the New Testament world, the heart was regarded as the center of thought. In modern times, we tend to regard it as the center of emotions only.

There are many ways to think; and persons' diversity in thinking should be regarded as parts of a delightful variety of the human experience. (1) There is straight-line, logical thinking that images a problem, gives it formal structure, and draws conclusions about it. This way of thinking works from cause to effect. It employs mathematical precision. It is called *deduction.* Engineers could draw plans for a bridge on the deductions they can make. (2) A second way of thinking is to observe a situation that already exists, to explore why it exists, to take it apart and see how it works. This way of thinking is called *induction.* Biologists and the medical sciences observe the human body by the process of induction. This way of thinking involves analysis and experimentation. It looks for what makes things tick. (3) There is thinking that puts together ideas and mental pictures that are neither logical nor previously existing. This way of thinking is called *creative thinking.* This method is used by poets, artists, and even historians who try to explain what events mean. This method of thinking draws on human experience and relationships and stresses differing ways of putting them all together.

A technological society prizes those forms of thought that produce machines, consumer goods, and laborsaving mechanical devices. A humane society welcomes the forms of thought that promote health care and the well-being and comfort of persons. An academic society stresses the forms of thinking that produce literature, provide artistic creations, and encourage reflection. It is a fact drawn from experience that all persons do not think alike. Nor are all persons equally skilled in various ways of thinking. It is a sad commentary on thinking persons that they do not learn to appreciate and value ways of thinking other than their own. For example, a father who is successful in business should not scorn a son who is an artist. Nor should a musician be impatient with a farmer who produces food but does not care for certain musical compositions. A smart person may have mastered one type of thinking. A wise person will see value in all ways of reflection and value their possibilities.

RELIGIOUS MAN

Worship is a universal experience. Primitive man faced with the awe of the world about him responded with worship.[7] When persons reflect about the grandeur of what lies outside of them, they experience the holy and are moved to worship.[8] Worship may be done superstitiously, and it may be given an idolatrous expression (Rom. 1:19–21). Yet the capacity for worship and the necessity to worship are traits that distinguish people from animals. Mankind is incurably religious. In his sermon at Athens (Acts 17:16–31), Paul paid tribute to the religious nature of the Greeks.

Christians must not forget that it is a person's religious impulse that makes possible true worship as well as false worship. True worship is distinguished from false worship not by the impulse or motivation of the worshiper but by the object worshiped. It is a paradox of our existence that the source of our deepest expression is also the possibility of our greatest distortion.

PERSONAL LEARNING ACTIVITY 9
Study Isaiah 40:18–20 and Isaiah 6:1–8. Write a paragraph that contrasts false worship and true worship.

Religious man should bring all of his capacities to bear on his religious commitment. We do not worship merely with our minds. Spiritual concerns always have some tangible bodily expression. Just as our toolmaking abilities, the possibilities for play, and the processes of thought involve total participation, even so our capacity for worship includes all of each of us. Worship is not done without bodies nor without places in which worship is experienced. Places of worship may be of all sorts, not merely buildings designated for that purpose. Worship is not done without reflection. We may go through prescribed rituals; but without thinking of their meaning and concentrating on the object of worship, there is no worship.

Worship may be a special possibility for persons, but it is not performed by only one part of our being. Worship is a total and consuming task.

CONCLUSION

If life is to be lived to its fullest, all of man's particular abilities must be interrelated and concentrated in his every act. Satisfying work involves an element of renewal and creative play; it requires the concentration of our minds; and, when done before God, it is an act of worship. The biblical prayer that acknowledges this is the request that God will bless and establish the work of our hands (Ps. 90:17).

Genuine play involves effort, concentration, and a joyful spirit before the Lord. Psalm 100 is a biblical expression associated with the festivals of Israel. Genuine and fruitful thinking is hard work; it is best accomplished by a relaxed and creative mind; and it ought to be challenged by the limitless mystery and impetus of religious reflection. The wisdom literature of the Old Testament is a good example of such thinking. See especially the book of Proverbs. The true worshiper should bring some gift of the product of his labors. The joy of celebration is a necessary part of worship as is the best effort of our minds. A dramatic picture of the work of true worship is Revelation 4. This is how it ought to be. All of each of us should be involved totally in an integrated way in everything we do. But that is not the way things are. Life is fragmented; our efforts are divided. We know that the God-given responsibility for our wholeness has been used irresponsibly. The image of God within us is no longer intact. We view the self we are supposed to be in the faded mirror of what we actually are.

NOTES

1. See *Science Year: The World Book Science Annual* (Chicago: Field Enterprises Educational Corporation, 1977), pp. 224–54.

2. For a well-researched view of primitive agricultural life, see Alex Haley, *Roots* (New York: The Doubleday Co., 1976), pp. 1–126.

3. D. B. J. Campbell, *The Old Testament for Modern Readers* (Atlanta: John Knox Press, 1972), p. 104. Used by permission.

4. See Gordon Dahl, *Work, Play, and Worship in a Leisure-Oriented Society* (Minneapolis: Augsburg Publishing House, 1972); Michael J.

Ellis, *Why People Play* (Englewood Cliffs, N.J.: Prentice-Hall, 1973); Max Kaplan, ed., *Technology, Human Values, and Leisure* (Nashville: Abingdon Press, 1971).

5. Wayne Oates, *Confessions of a Workaholic* (New York: World Publishing Co., 1971).

6. William L. Hendricks, "Leisure" (Chapel address at Southwestern Baptist Theological Seminary, Fort Worth, Texas, April 6, 1976).

7. Compare the works of Mircea Eliade, both his early *Patterns of Comparative Religion* (New York: Sheed and Ward, 1958) and his latest *Histoire des Croyances et des Idees religieuses,* Vol. 1, *De L'age de Pieree aux mysteras d Eleusis* (Paris: Payot, 1976).

8. Rudolf Otto, *The Idea of the Holy* (New York: Oxford University Press, 1958).

Chapter 4
The Image and the Likeness

In our home, built in the 1920s, are two toothbrush sinks. Toothbrush sinks are small sinks, on the wall, exclusively used for dental hygiene. Because of the passing of time and plumbing problems, they no longer work; but they do make good planters. However, there is in an old house nearby one toothbrush sink that does work and that does fulfill its intended function well. There is an element of pathos in seeing anything that does not fulfill its intended purpose. Man was made as a distinct and novel creation of God intended to find fulfillment and glorify God. But we are no longer working at what God intended. The image of God in us no longer functions as it was intended. There is a model of what man is supposed to be. There is one in whom the image of God is undiminished—one who is what all men are supposed to be. That one is Jesus Christ. He is a working model of what we should be.

Chapter 3 suggested that work and play are acts that both man and animals have in common. Thought and worship are acts that only persons can do. This chapter explores (1) what the image of God in persons means, (2) how the image is altered by our fallenness, (3) the results of sin on God's image in us, and (4) one person in whom the true image remains intact.

The Second Commandment forbids the making of idols. The reason idols are forbidden is that no created thing can capture the identity of God. But God himself has revealed his own identity in his Son Jesus who is the very image of God (Heb. 1:3). Jesus came to us as a person (Heb. 1:14). We should expect, therefore, to find some similarity between our personhood and God. Genesis puts the matter concisely by stating that male and female persons are made in the image and likeness of God. In these statements the Bible affirms that people are special because they are related to God in a special way. The term *image of*

God is the biblical and theological way of speaking of man's distinctiveness. The term is a controversial one, and it must be defined carefully. Although the term *image of God* does not occur often in the Bible, the idea is a necessary one to relate man to God and to define the distinctiveness of personhood.

Since people's distinctiveness from all the rest of creation is that they are made in God's image, it is important to say what that image is. The task is made difficult because the Bible itself does not define the image.

PERSONAL LEARNING ACTIVITY 10
Before reading further, use the concordance in your Bible to find and read all the references to the image of God. Then write a paragraph explaining what you feel the term means.

Some people assert that the image must be a literal image. They argue that it is apparent what is meant when one says of a son that he is the "image of his father." This means physical likeness. Those who hold this view affirm that God is basically physical and has a shape and that God is the pattern for the way they are designed physically.[1]

Classical Christianity has a great problem with saying that the image of God in man is man's physical makeup, or his upright position. The Bible has much to say about God's existence being different from our own. God is Spirit (John 4:24). His thoughts are not our thoughts nor his ways our ways (Isa. 55:8). No man has seen God at any time (John 1:18). The Old Testament does speak of God as having arms, feet, eyes, and so on; but this is understood as human language used to describe God who is not bound by our human limitations. The Bible is explicit that God's dimension is not physical like ours. The new heaven and the new earth promised in Revelation are new creations that redeem our present existence. They are not merely physical rearrangements that extend it. For these biblical reasons we must reject the idea that the image of God in persons is a physical image. If God were physical, how could he be present in all times and places (Ps. 139)? Christian theology must not picture people as puppets cut from a master pattern of a physical God. Nor can we image God as a version of a human merely drawn to a large scale.

A more acceptable view of the image of God in man is that the image is a person's reasoning ability. Such people as Augustine, Aquinas, and Calvin have interpreted the image in this way.[2] There are many reasons to believe that our ability to reason is what separates us from all other created existence. The Bible assumes that man can think, know, respond, and reason things out. (Only people buy life insurance because only they are troubled about dying and are farsighted enough to make provisions for loved ones.) The Old Testament asks men to reason together about the fact that God has offered to make their lives, tainted by sin, as white as snow (Isa. 1:18). The New Testament encourages Christians to "have the mind of Christ" (1 Cor. 2:16).

There are some problems in defining the image of God in man as knowledge or the ability to reason. In addition to the ability to reason, human personhood involves emotional and volitional and social elements. If we understood reason to mean the ability to reflect rationally on abstract problems, those who have higher intellectual ability or more formal education would be more in the image of God than less clever or less educated persons. Such is not the case. There is no essential correlation between brilliance, education, or mental skills and the image of God. The Bible affirms that all people are made in God's image. The capacity for thinking and reflection is related to the image of God in man. Nevertheless, it is problematic to suggest that reason is the best way to define the image. In one way this view reduces the image of God to a portion of man's ability, and in another way it fosters spiritual pride, particularly among those who are proud of their intellectual attainments.

PERSONAL LEARNING ACTIVITY 11
Review Personal Learning Activity 10 and make any changes you feel you should make in the paragraph you have written.

We need a definition of the image of God in man by which all of every person is included. The following definition captures what the Bible means. *The image of God in persons is the potentiality, ability, and responsibility to respond to God, the self, and others.* This definition includes a person's thinking abilities. It also includes the emotional and volitional aspects of our being. The idea of potentiality includes infants and those mentally unable to give a full, reasoned response to God. Even if the potentiality of being able to respond to God in a reflective way is never brought to full ability (as in those who die in infancy or those whose mental abilities never develop), we may say they are yet in the image of God and are under his covenant mercy.

The above definition also includes the necessary social relationships of our human existence. Male and female are created with the possibility of being complementary. People are made in such a way that they can love themselves and reflect on their own well-being before God. As stated in chapters 1 and 2, persons are inevitably interrelated to and are dependent on other persons in all areas of life. The ability to relate to God, the self, and others is the image of God in man. This ability carries with it the responsibility to relate to God, the self, and the others. Ideally, our relationships should be good. Realistically, they are not. Something is wrong. We have denied our responsibility.

RESPONSIBILITY DENIED

God gave men the ability to respond. God made all things good. Therefore man's response to God, the self, and others should be good. But it is often hostile, bad, and ugly. Man has denied his responsibility. When something moves from a higher good for which it is intended to a lower place or state for which it is not intended, we describe that movement with the crisis word *fall.* Genesis 3 is the story of the fall of man from where God intended him to be to a state where he was not intended to be. Without the tragic account of the fall, the remainder of the Bible would not make sense. No fall—no redemption; no sin—no salvation. Only God can reverse the effects of a previous action. In Jesus he is reversing the fall.[3] What the Bible says of Adam must be said of all persons. We have not fulfilled God's intention for ourselves. We have "come short of the glory of God" (Rom. 3:23). We are fallen. And our fallenness is that we have denied and distorted the responsibility to respond to God, to self, and to others. The theological name for this denial and distortion is sin.

To account for sin, the Bible speaks of an outside temptation to sin, the evil one. It also speaks of a willingness on our part to cooperate in sin. Paul called this condition the flesh. John called the fallen condition of existence around us the world. Christian theology has summarized our problem in fallenness in these three terms: the evil one, flesh, and the world. The Bible pictures the foes of mankind through these terms.

In Genesis 3 the possibilities for sin and the consequences of sin are pictured dramatically. Adam and Eve refused to respond with obedience to God. They rejected the command not to eat of the tree of knowledge. This is responsibility denied. Our lives mirror that pattern. We respond to God with disobedience and the rejection of his claim to be God. We want to be as gods. We have denied the responsibility to respond in goodness to God, the source of all good.

In their guilt, Adam and Eve hid from God. The dilemma of all human life is trying to hide our weaknesses from others. We try to deceive even ourselves about who we are, how we feel, where we have failed. In short, we try to justify ourselves. When persons attempt to justify themselves, they deny that "it is God who justifies" (Rom. 8:33, RSV). It is a mark of our fallenness that we do not respond to ourselves in goodness and in truth. Disobedience is the first shape of responsibility denied. Self-justification is the second shape of responsibility denied.

Our fallenness also separates us from the good relationship God intended persons to have with one another. This breakdown of fellowship is seen particularly in Adam's blaming Eve for his disobedience. Accusations and blaming others result in alienation from them. We all deny our responsibility for others and to others when we blame them for what we ourselves are responsible. Surely one of the ways in which Christianity undoes the fall is to help each person accept responsibility for himself/herself. It is a further evidence of Christian concern that we are not to blame others. Rather we are to feel responsible for them that their lives and ours might have the good response God intended them to have.

The fall is the denial of responsibility. But denying responsibility does not do away with the fact of our responsibility. Our denial and distortion of the good responses we should make to God and life make life fallen and sinful. Something has happened to the image of God in us because we have refused to make the good responses to God, to ourselves, and to others.

THE CRACKED MIRROR

Our lives were intended to be a mirror of the goodness of God. God's image in Adam and in us was intended to be a positive response. However, the mirror is cracked. The image is marred. All we see of God in our disobedient selves is a mere shadow of what he is and of what we are intended to be. We need to assess the extent of the damage before we can estimate the repairs and ask about a replacement.

Partial Depravity Theory

A large segment of the Christian community has read Genesis 1:26 to mean that unfallen man has two things from God—an image and a likeness. The likeness was the possibility to live forever, the ability not to suffer, and the ability to control our passions. According to this view, the likeness was lost or distorted in the fall. The image, which was unfallen man's reasoning ability to reflect on and deserve God, was not damaged essentially by the fall. *Partial depravity* is an unfortunate term that means man's ability to find God is affected only partly by sin. This view asserts that fallen man's reason is not affected essentially by his sin and that his reason can discover God.

There are two problems with this view. (1) It is based on an incorrect interpretation of Genesis 1:26. Image and likeness are two different ways of saying the same thing. (2) Both Scriptures and the experiences of life illustrate that our minds are as affected by sin as is any other part of us. Rather than reasoning our way to God, we distort his revelation (Rom. 1:18 to 3:23).

Total Depravity Theory

A second view of the extent of damage to the mirror of God's image in us is less optimistic. But it is more realistic because it fits the biblical explanation and the actual circumstances. This second view asserts that all of every person is affected by sin. The mirror of God in persons is cracked badly and requires a radical repair. As fallen persons our reason may discover the marvels of technology and invent all kinds of machinery to make life easier. But the tragic history of mankind, illustrated by the tragedy of two global wars and countless military hostilities in our own century, shows that we have not discovered by our unaided reason the power to make us good and help us live in peace.

It is precisely our cleverness and strong reasoning abilities that we have used to destroy one another and thereby to deny the image of God in us and in one another. Romans 1:18 to 3:23 is a powerful expression about how persons use their reasons to distort and deny the reality of God. This second view of what happened to the image in the fall is called *total depravity*. This term is even more unfortunate than *partial depravity*. It is more unfortunate because some people have used or have understood the term *total depravity* to mean that people cannot do anything good in any area of life. This interpretation is false and misleading. All persons are given varieties of good gifts by God and hold varieties of good gifts from God. Persons may be strong, creative, friendly, and helpful to others regardless of their religious commitments. Total depravity means that no person can find God unless God takes the initiative and makes possible the good response man should give to God. Total depravity means that even our reason, and perhaps especially our reason, is affected by sin in the matter of finding God.

If one takes the view that fallen humanity does not reflect the image of God but rather distorts it, two further things must be said. (1) There is some reflection of the image of God that still shines through every person and makes him/her valuable. Even in a fallen state, we have not lost our capacity for God. (2) Somewhere an ideal is required—an ideal that will illustrate what the image of God in man ought to be and is intended to be ultimately. That true image cannot be Adam, because all Adams, including the first Adam, are fallen.

THE TRUE IMAGE

God rejects all images made by men in order to give us the true image of himself. The beauty of the gospel is that God's own image of himself came "in the likeness of sinful flesh" (Rom. 8:3).

Yet he was without sin (Heb. 4:15), but he became sin for us, that we might be declared righteous by God, through him. In substance, that is the heart of the Christian message.

The implications are radical. The second Adam has recreated the image of God for us even as first Adam has distorted it for us. We are involved responsibly in both parts of the process. When we choose the old Adam by inevitable necessity of birth and circumstance, the image of God is shattered in us. When we choose the new Adam by the possibility of grace, the image of God is being restored in us.

Hebrews 1:3 is an important New Testament reference about Christ's being the true image of God. "He reflects the glory of God and bears the very stamp of his nature, upholding the universe by his word of power" (RSV). The term translated *very stamp of* was the word used of an impression left in wax by a signet ring or stamp. Jesus has the very seal of God. He is the true image of God. It is necessary at some point for us to have a clear clue to the nature of God. It is also necessary for us to have an undistorted view of what mankind is intended to be. The union is brought about in Jesus Christ. He is both true God and true man. He is the image of God, and he is capable of restoring the shattered image of God in all persons.

It is necessary to keep speaking about Christ at every point in our discussion about man. This is so because God has shown us in the person of Jesus Christ who man is, and who man is intended to be.

It is necessary also to speak of Christ in a Christian discussion of the nature of mankind. God has granted glimpses of himself in the promise of the Old Testament and its witness to Christ. He also has let himself be seen in the fulfillment of the New Testament and its proclamation of the Christ event. In other words, God gives mankind a continuing witness about God and about mankind. As Jesus is the Word of God, so also he is a word about men.

The humanity of Jesus bears the stamp of what God intends for persons to be. Romans 8:29 says it is God's will that persons should "be conformed to the image of his Son, that he might be the firstborn among many brethren." In the midst of our brokenness, Christ is a promise of wholeness. When we want to see what God is like, we look to Christ. When we want to see what personhood is intended to be, we also look to Christ.

SUMMARY

Man's distinctiveness is that he is created in the image of God. Mankind's tragedy is that we have distorted the image of God in us. God's intention was that his image in us should bring forth the good response to God, ourselves, and others. Because of a traumatic fall, each of us rejects the responsibility of the good response. In this rejection, the image is shattered. In God's persistent and patient goodness, we are given a picture of what it means to be in God's image. That picture is Christ. Not only is he the picture of God's image, he also is the possibility of God's image being restored in each of us.

God has a consuming desire for wholeness. He intended us to be whole persons, and it is the totality of our personhood he intends to redeem. Each person is distinctive in some ways. Every person is responsible to God. We must stand for this wholeness and in this responsibility. However much we seem to be fragmented and separated by sin, by death, by our rebellion, in God's sight we are whole persons; and he will deal with our totality even in its fragmentation. Chapter 5 will take up the problem of our wholeness versus our seeming fragmentation.

PERSONAL LEARNING ACTIVITY 12

Write your own definition of the following terms as they would be used in a discussion of sin: partial depravity, total depravity, evil one, flesh, world.

NOTES

1. Compare Walter Martin, *The Kingdom of the Cults* (Grand Rapids: Zondervan Publishing House, 1965), pp. 93–96.
2. See Alan Richardson, "Doctrine of Man," *A Dictionary of Christian Theology* (Philadelphia: The Westminster Press, 1969), pp. 202–205.
3. Irenaeus. *The Demonstration of Apostolic Preaching.*

Chapter 5

My Soul and Body

All day I have been blessed by the beauty in Callaway Gardens, Georgia. It is early spring, and the crocuses, wild plums, and forsythias are a riot of blooms. On the table before me are two full-formed jonquils picked by friends from clumps beside the road. I marvel at their intricacy. The blossoms are the body of the flowers' beauty. Yet without the green stems and leaves that nourished them, and without the bulb and roots from which they emerged, they would not be. People are like that too. We are made up of various dimensions—physical, psychological, social, and spiritual—but we are total selves.

"Getting it all together" is a way of saying that people want wholeness. The Bible speaks of persons as being fearfully and wonderfully made. Anatomy illustrates the complexity of the human makeup. Modern medicine with its large number of specialties acknowledges the reality that each person is a varied and diverse individual with several physical systems.

The remarkable part of this diversity is that each portion carries out its function so that the entire individual can act. It is astonishing how many different muscles, brain waves, acts of motor reflexes, and decisions of the will a person must make to cross the street. We are aware of the deficiency only when some part is not functioning. With all our thousands of parts, impulses, and reflexes, we are intended to function as whole persons.

Young people speak of "having it all together." Not to have it all together is to be fragmented. To be fragmented is to be unable to do what we are intended to do. This is the paradox and the irony of our predicament. We are supposed to have it all together—all of life should fit together harmoniously and happily. But something unhealthy abounds in our world and in us as individuals. This chapter must express both the ideal and the actual. As God's creation, we are total persons; but we find our lives are not functioning freely and fully as they should. At the physical level, there are the limitations of disease and death. At the psychological level, there is a disorder and confusion. At the spiritual level, there is a divided self. Our problem is that something bad has disrupted the unity of the whole persons we were intended to be.

The first part of this chapter will examine the popular and destructive notion that persons come in parts and that one part is good and another bad. A plea based on the Bible and experience will be made for the unity for which we were created and which we need so much. The second part will explore how various Bible words fit into this pattern of unity. The third division of the chapter will deal with how and why we are fragmented. The fourth section will return to Jesus Christ, the model of the unified person which we are intended to be and the full salvation he brings. This chapter will repeat the cycle of our existence and the threefold pattern of this book: what we are intended to be (unity), what we actually are (fragmented), and what we can become through Jesus Christ (a full unity).

PERSONAL LEARNING ACTIVITY 13
Complete this activity before studying further. Below are four words you have read many times in your Bible. Write what you think the biblical meaning of each is.

body

soul

spirit

flesh

THE ANGEL IN THE SLOT MACHINE

The most pervasive division of persons in religious circles is body and soul. It is easy to affirm that some biblical references suggest this division.

An alternative type of division is the threefold division suggested in 1 Thessalonians 5:23. According to this theory there are three parts of man, and the different parts have almost independent ways of relating to God and to the world. This verse generally has been understood in the light of Greek thinking which taught that man had a body and a soul. The powerful gnostic currents from New Testament days to the present have suggested that the body is sinful because it is composed of matter—the opposite of spirit. The following quotation from a gnostic source illustrates this idea clearly. "The Soul once turned toward matter, she became enamored of it, and burning with the desire to experience the pleasures of the body, she no longer wanted to disengage herself from it. Thus the world was born." [1]

Puritanism, or at least the popular picture we have of puritanism, continues this dichotomy of persons. (Dichotomy means that there are two parts of a thing. In this instance the parts would be body and soul.) The experience of death seems to reenforce this two-part view of persons. Anyone observing a death is aware that the principle which gives life is gone. Basic chemistry attests that all beings disintegrate when the life principle is gone. Therefore, the part of us that is with God after this life is other than the body. So go the arguments for the two- or three-part theories of persons.

There are several problems with a two-part theory of persons. (1) There is usually the assumption that the body or the physical part of a person is sinful because it is material. This marks off matter as evil and makes sinfulness the result of having a physical body. Therefore, to be born is to be sinful. To experience physical pleasure is wrong. To take any awareness of man's pressing physical needs is not a spiritual type of ministry. The body-is-bad syndrome keeps churches from ministering to whole persons. The denial of the body becomes a religious obligation. Frustrations abound in the body-is-bad view. For whether we like it or not, we cannot serve God without our bodies. (2) The two-part view of persons usually suggests that soul or spirit is good. The goal becomes otherworldly. Salvation of the soul may be caricatured as some inner spiritual affirmation that does not affect the body or one's tangible actions in this life. The material of creation and of people's own bodies is to be downgraded or expended without any qualms. To be spiritual means not to pay attention to the body.

The error is obvious. It is not possible to deny any facet of the self. Suppressing one aspect of our being brings serious problems. To assign the wrongs of persons to the body and to assert that the spirit is pure is what I call the-angel-in-the-slot-machine view of personhood. That is, there is something pure and precious inside a dull, heavy machine. This view denies the value of the body and distorts the relationship of body and soul.

A certain kind of ultimate pride comes in a form of dualism that speaks of the immortality of the soul. This extreme view supposes that the soul or spirit of a person is a portion of God himself. This view is opposed to the firm biblical insight that God creates and permits all life. God alone has the ultimate power of life and death. Just as he creates the possibility of life after death, he grants us the gift of life before death. Our times are in his hands. People are taught to fear no one nor to reverence any person unduly. Rather we are to "fear [reverence] him who is able to destroy both soul and body [the total person] in hell" (Matt. 10:28, ASV). Connected with the idea of the automatic immortality of the pure soul is the supposition that man's spirit does not sin. According to this view, it is the body that sins. Suicide is the ultimate answer to this kind of dualism that plays off a sinless spirit against a gross sinful body. If our bodies are our problem, we should get rid of them. If we are sinless souls imprisoned in sinful bodies, be done with the body. This solution is absurd, and it leads to much mischief under the guise of spiritual living. Even though we are puzzled by physical death, and even though some persons may interpret certain Scriptures to mean that people come in parts, we cannot uphold the-angel-in-the-slot-machine view of man's being.

THE TOTALITY OF PERSONS—FOUR LITTLE WORDS

We are people of many parts, but all of the parts are designed to function as a whole. The integration or fitting together of all life into a harmonious whole is God's intention for persons. Genesis 1—3 expresses this totality of the individual. The dust of earth and the breath of God are mixed to provide a total life. Four different levels or dimensions of life are discernible, but all of these levels and dimensions involve a body to express themselves *(the physical dimension).* They all involve an inner consciousness, dependent on the physical structure of the mind to reflect on themselves *(the psychological dimension).* They all involve the presence of others and an awareness of living in communities of tangible people to express themselves *(the social dimension).* All levels of life are required to worship and to be aware of the measure and measuring of ultimate reality *(the spiritual dimension).* What we think reflects who we are; how we act tells about body awareness and requires physical energy. The soul or ultimate dimension expresses the depth of who we are. This view of a multidimensional total person is documented both from Scriptures and from life. A careful definition of four words will help to comprehend the wholeness of persons.

Body

If you ask someone to check an empty room, you expect the response, "There's no*body* there." *Body,* the physical dimension of persons, is the first and indispensable way of knowing about any*body.* Body is the shape a being is. All persons and things have shape, size, density. The combination of these is called *body.* It is inconceivable to think of friends or loved ones without reflecting on their forms or what they have done with their bodies. The Old Testament took for granted the fact that all beings were shaped. There is no specific Old Testament word for body. There are a variety of ways of expressing what body is about. A living body is called "a living soul" (Gen. 2:7). Dead bodies are called corpses. All bodies are weak; they are flesh. Go not to the Egyptians for they "are men, and not God; their horses flesh, and not spirit" (Isa. 31:3).

It may have been assumed by the Greeks that spirit was formless. But Paul spoke with clarity of spiritual bodies (1 Cor. 15). The Bible ascribes form to God—the arm of the Lord, the eyes of the Lord, and so on. Such speech is an accommodation to men by describing God in human language. But something deeper is implied also. There is nothing where there is no*body.* Even the realm of spirit is embodied. There are physical forms and spiritual forms, but nothing is conceivable without a form. John 4:24 says that God is Spirit. This verse expresses the dimension of his existence. It does not preclude spiritual form. If Christians are to image Christ as risen Lord, they must in some sense ascribe to him body or form. All of this is to say that body is essential to being. Body is not the cause of sin. Furthermore Christians await the resurrection of the body. Shape and size are necessary dimensions of existence. One cannot be appropriately Christian and downgrade or ignore the body. For the body is the temple (form) in which God dwells and has lordship among people. "Know ye not that ye are the temple of God" (1 Cor. 3:16). We are to yield our bodies to God. "I appeal to you therefore, brethren, by the mercies of God, to present your bodies as a living sacrifice, holy and acceptable to God, which is your spiritual worship" (Rom. 12:1, RSV). It was by Christ's body that we were redeemed (1 Pet. 2:24). We cannot say we are sinful because we have bodies. Nor can we say we can serve God or help others without some form for doing so. The bodily dimension of persons is the most recognizable and primary of all ways of being. The body is not a part of us; it is the shape we are.

Soul

A second term to help us describe ourselves is *soul.* The dualist view seems to assume that the soul is some inner-zippered lining of a body that comes out and floats about. The word for soul in the Old Testament and in the New Testament is best understood to mean the *total self.* Soul is the whole of who we are, and this includes the form or body in which we are shaped. It is true that soul often refers to the dimension of man that is the inner self—the reflective and feeling element of persons. This use of soul to reflect the inner man is a synonym for spirit, which will be described in the next section. But soul is normally used to mean the total self. When the psalmist cried, "No man cared for my soul" (Ps. 142:4), he meant that no one was concerned about him, all or any part of him. Ezekiel 18:4, " 'Behold, all souls are mine; the soul of the father as well as the soul of the son is mine: the soul that sins shall die' " (RSV), cannot be distorted to mean that an inner, ghostly form belongs to God, and he does not care for man's body. A soul is a total self. A body is a part of every self. The latter part of Ezekiel 18:4 speaks of souls sinning and therefore dying. This sinning is not accomplished without a body or form. Jesus gave his life (the Greek word is soul) for his sheep (John 10:11). *Soul* is the best term to describe the totality

The fitting together of all of life into a harmonious whole is God's intention for persons. Personhood cannot be divided into many little parts and tucked away into separate compartments.

of an individual when we want to speak of his or her entire person and not just the physical exterior. Soul is not an interior part of persons, but it describes both the form of a person and a dimension of reflecting and feeling which goes on within that person.

To know that soul equals self has far-reaching consequences. To be soul-winners means to relate all of persons to God. Soul-winning has to do with every dimension of the individual. Those who understand what it is to be a saved soul cannot divorce evangelism and ethics. To have your soul saved speaks about proper physical and mental obedience to God in this life, as well as the deliverance of the whole person in the world to come. All souls (people) are indeed God's, and he truly cares for our souls (us). The biblical unitary view of the person keeps us from cutting off evangelism and from ignoring ethics. This is God's world. We are his people. He wants to save his entire creation, and he wants to save all of each of us.

Spirit

The third word in a biblical view of personhood is *spirit.* In dualism spirit is often contrasted to body. There are many biblical uses of spirit. Sometimes spirit and soul are synonyms to express an ultimate dimension of man and his concerns. In some instances spirit seems to be an almost physical substance that comes upon people, causing them to do unusual and special kinds of things. This view of spirit lies behind the Old Testament ideas about the early, ecstatic prophets and the New Testament references about the Spirit of God in Acts.

Spirit is also defined in the Bible as that breath of God in persons that relates them to God and is indestructible because God will not permit it to be destroyed by death. This understanding of spirit lies behind Isaiah 38:16; Ecclesiastes 12:7; and John 19:30. Sometimes spirit is a personified evil that is neither of persons nor of God. Such are the evil spirits (1 Sam. 16:23) and the lying spirits (1 Kings 22:22–23; 2 Chron. 18:21–22). We have already referred to John 4:24 and interpreted that reference to God as Spirit as meaning that spirit is the dimension and realm of God's existence.

In this maze of definitions of spirit, it is important to return to the root idea of the word. The Old Testament word for spirit and the New Testament term basically mean wind, breath, power, force, animating principle. Spirit is the force by which God acts. Spirit is the power of God, the inner essence of his being. This is true also of persons. "God has revealed to us through the Spirit. For the Spirit searches everything, even the depths of God. For what person knows a man's thoughts except the spirit of the man which is in him? So also no one comprehends the thoughts of God except the Spirit of God" (1 Cor. 2:10–11, RSV). Spirit is not a part of man; it is the inner essence of man's existence. It is one dimension of his being. Spirit is the aspect of man that is most like God. Spirit is an expression of the self; and spirit is the animating force of the body. A good theological definition of spirit is that energizing capacity of man that cooperates with the Spirit of God to order all of life in God's ways. Paul's phrase "to walk after the Spirit" expresses a way of channeling all of life by God's strength into ways that are godly. But the walk "in the spirit" is complicated by our fourth term—*flesh.*

Flesh

In its biological dimension, flesh is the chemical composition of man. In its moral dimension, flesh is the point of weakness that permits moral lapses. In its theological dimension, flesh is the capacity to cooperate with the evil one and the demonic pressures of the world about us.

Just as spirit is sometimes a synonym for soul, flesh is sometimes a synonym for body. But neither flesh nor spirit refers to a part of a person. Rather, they refer to the direction the entire self takes. Flesh is weak, but it is not necessarily sinful, for Christ became flesh (John 1:14). There is a more negative view of flesh in Paul's writings than in John's. Paul wrote: "God has done what the law, weakened by the flesh, could not do: sending his own Son in the likeness of sinful flesh and for sin, he condemned sin in the flesh" (Rom. 8:3, RSV).

As it is used most often in the Bible, flesh is not so much the chemicals that compose the body. It is the weakness and finitude bodies exhibit. Flesh is not meat on bones; it is the capacity to walk away from God.

Flesh is the opposite of spirit. It is not any particular part of us. It is the capacity for a wrong use of our total selves. Although *walking after the Spirit* means channeling all of life by God's strength into ways that are God's, *walking after the flesh* means to order all of life according to the evil one.

Summary

Persons are total beings (selves/souls); they are formed in bodies. Within each of us and demonstrated by the corporate experience of all persons, there are warring capacities of flesh and spirit that are attitudes and postures out of which life is lived. God created man with many parts and capacities—physical, psychological, and spiritual. All of these parts are individual and indispensable facets of a larger whole. Persons are intended to be whole selves. Man's physical being should be in harmony with his psychological and spiritual being. When all of life is not together, there is illness, death, confusion, and fragmentation. Unfortunately, this latter description is how it is with us. But it should not be so. The next section of this book will describe the extent to which all dimensions of our lives are distorted and fragmented by sin.

PERSONAL LEARNING ACTIVITY 14

Review your definitions of the words in Personal Learning Activity 13. Write a paragraph stating a new or different idea you have learned about each. Then explain why you agree or disagree with each idea.

"COME, YE SINNERS, POOR AND NEEDY"

"Come, Ye Sinners, Poor and Needy" is an old Southern folk hymn sung often by our forefathers. To some congregations today it has lost its longing appeal because of its supposedly negative view of man. There are such phrases as "weak and wounded, sick and sore," "come, ye weary, heavy laden, lost and ruined by the fall." Our society has suppressed emotion in religion. Good public relations has taught us to put our best foot forward. Indeed we are to pretend that there are no flaws, no problems. But there is no point in supposing all is well with us, for it is not so. There are many things wrong with our existence. The religious word for what is wrong with existence is *sin*. One reason people so much resist the designation *sinner* today is because of definitions of sin that use only moral categories. The next chapter will give a full definition of sin. This section gives only a provisional definition of evil and a description of its consequences for our total selves.

Evil is the opposite of good. Evil is that which brings death, decay, and fragmentation. Evil is that which pulls apart the total self and separates it from God, from others, and from its own intended wholeness. To review this chapter and to preview the next chapter, reflect on this definition of evil and express how this broader view of evil differs from moral definitions of sinfulness. Decide why it is helpful to distinguish natural calamities from sinful actions for which we as individuals are responsible.

At the biological level evil affects all of us by disease, decay, and finally death. We cannot assert, of course, that germs and physical illness come to every individual because of deliberate acts of sin. Illness and pain are wrong and undesirable because they are not what God desires for us, and they are conditions from which he will ultimately deliver us. The book of Job teaches us plainly that individuals are not always responsible for the tragedies that come to them. But we also cannot overlook the fact that abusing our bodies or failing to care for them is a form of sin with inevitable evil consequences. We can speak of death and disease as evil because they do not express God's ultimate intentions for his creation. He wills life and health. Evil is expressed in death and lack of health. Our physical problems and our mortality are parts of evil and are aggravated by our own individual sinfulness in matters of health. To see this is to understand how sinfulness as a part of evil affects the total life of each person and affects the corporate life of mankind. The New Testament shows a profound insight by relating even physical problems to the kingdom of evil.

The twentieth century is the century of the study of the mind. Since the rise of psychology as a formal science in the late nineteenth century, with the work of Wilhelm Wundt, seven major fields of psychological studies have developed. Psychologists study human and animal behavior and work with the full range of human responses and thought. Clinical psychologists have observed that human personality, as well as the physical body, undergoes disorder and disease. These disorders may be caused by the individual actions of the person, by the family setting, or by the larger social context. Often all three causes contribute to psychological illness. Certain areas of modern medical practice demonstrate that people are whole selves whose entire selves are affected by their own actions and the acts of other people. The trend of modern medicine to view persons as whole selves is a good parallel to the theological understanding that we are intended to be integrated persons before God.

Just as we cannot assign all physical illness to sinful acts of the individual, we cannot assign in every instance all mental and emotional problems that individuals undergo to acts of the individuals. But the result of mental and emotional illness is evil. For these forms of illness, like our physical problems, do not reflect God's perfect intention for his creation. The main point to remember is that physical problems affect the total person, and so do mental or psychological problems.

Theological fragmentation is seen in rebellion against God, a resistance to life and the good that God intends for us. Theological illness is a being lost from God, the source of our own being. It is rebellion against God who desires only that which is good for his creation. All of life is affected by sin. Unhealthy spiritual conditions as well as biological and psychological disorders reflect the condition of evil in our existence. Sin is a condition that is experienced individually. It is also a larger social problem that affects all persons and the entire world. There is a tendency among some Christians to view all sin and evil as the result of the individuals' acts of immorality and personal sin. This is not the case. Sin and evil have broad social and corporate affects on people who did not directly cause them, nor are they responsible for them. Examples of sin and evil that are experienced at the social level are wars, famines, and the denial of human rights.

By this time two things should be clear to the readers of this book and to those who try to reflect on all of life: (1) All of every person is affected by evil and sin and (2) the effects of sin and evil are not only individual, they are also social.

We have come to a difficult impasse. If all of each of us is affected by sin and evil and if sin and evil are social as well as individual, what hope is there for humanity? The only logical answer is to expect some kind of deliverance that will affect all individuals and the whole world which is now affected by sin and evil. Anything less will not do.

FULL SALVATION

We are total people. Each dimension of us affects all of us. There is something wrong with all of existence individually and collectively. That is the dark side of the picture. The bright side is that God who made the world is, in Jesus Christ, beginning to make the world right. The Christian community must live with the paradox that the light of God has begun to shine in Jesus Christ even in the midst of darkness. As the light grows brighter, the darkness seems heavier. This making right involves all of the world, and it involves all of each of us. We call this full salvation. Anything less than full salvation leaves off a part of what God desires for us.

PERSONAL LEARNING ACTIVITY 15

As you read the remainder of this chapter, make notes in the margin to identify things the Christian community can do to help others find full salvation.

Jesus' mighty works of healing demonstrated God's concern for the health of persons. Evil will persist until the end time. The wheat and tares will grow together (Matt. 13:24–30), but in the meantime the Christian community should, as much as possible, reflect the health God desires. Christians also should provide places of healing as evidence of their belief that God will heal all of the wounds of people.

Emotional and psychological well-being are also God's intention for us. Our minds, our wills, our hearts (in the popular sense of our emotions) should be healthy. One of the loveliest of Paul's benedictions is Philippians 4:7: "And the peace of God, which passeth all understanding, shall keep your hearts and minds through Christ Jesus." Good religion makes for good and positive mental health. A religious commitment that lingers only on guilt and is abnormally obsessed with blame and shame has not appropriated God's full salvation. Such persons often need help from both psychological and theological sources.

Salvation also knits back the deepest spiritual wounds of persons. The spiritual dimension of life is concerned with purpose, with ultimate relationship, with our well-being with God. When it is properly understood, spiritual salvation gives enormous resources to people at every level of their existence. We have our special religious vocabulary for spiritual salvation. But we must not suppose that our holy words apply only to some isolated part of life. The gift of grace has implications for all of every life and for the whole world.

God has measured salvation and grace with a larger measuring stick than sin and evil use. Grace abounds. As pervasive as sin and evil are, God's provision is more so. Paul captured this surplus of God's goodness in Romans 5:20. Chapters 7 and 8 of this book will explore further both God's gifts and our response to this surplus of grace.

SUMMARY

People are intended to be total persons. Their fragmentation comes from evil and sin. This chapter has seen us all together and has noted that, even in evil and sin, all are full persons because sin affects all of us. The next chapter will highlight the fragmentating nature of evil and sin.

NOTE

1. Quoted from the "Apocryphon of John," in Hans Jones, *The Gnostic Religion* (Boston: Beacon Press, 1958), p. 204.

Chapter 6

Evil and Sin

The fascinating world of underwater is a kind of glorious never-never land where marine life and the beauty of the underwater world can be observed in all of its natural coloration. But if the diver moves to a certain depth, the light from above becomes invisible; there is a silent darkness. Some divers report that this silent darkness is a warm, quiet retreat; others are frightened by it and swim toward the surface for reassurance. A diver diving alone without some instrument to measure his depth faces the grave peril of narcosis of the deep. Without any light, the diver becomes confused and cannot tell which direction is toward the light; when he thinks he is surfacing, he goes deeper until he runs out of oxygen or his lungs burst. It is a frightening prospect–swimming away from the light. It is a powerful parable of sin.

In chapter 5 we saw that every dimension of a person is related to the total being. Chapters 1 and 2 stated that all persons are related to one another. Chapter 9 will discuss the interrelations of all creation in God's redemption. All of these lines add up to a very complex picture. A good illustration of the interrelatedness of all existence is seen in the child's game of pickup sticks. A group of slender sticks, pointed at both ends, is held together and let fall into a heap. The object is to extract as many sticks as possible without causing any of the others to move. For even the player with the keenest eye and the steadiest hand, it is impossible to remove many individual sticks because they are all so closely related. That is also a parable of evil and sin.

PERSONAL LEARNING ACTIVITY 16
Before you study further, write your own explanation of the difference between evil and sin.

This chapter will take a closer look at what is wrong with

existence. The problem of existence has a two-focus view. These views are evil and sin.

EVIL

Evil is the larger designation of which sin is one particular category. Evil as a category includes sin as responsible human action; it also includes animal and human pain and suffering and natural calamities. In short, evil is anything that threatens, thwarts, or attempts to destroy any part of God's good creation. In its simplest definition, evil is the opposite of good. Augustine has defined evil as the absence of good. "For evil has no positive nature; but the loss of good has received the name 'evil.' " [1] Evil is determined by good, but it cannot overcome good ultimately. Evil is, in fact, self-destructive. Those things in creation that are opposed to God are self-destructive. It is not the nature of the creature to be evil. Evil is an unnatural thing. "The vice which makes those who are called His enemies resist Him, is an evil not to God, but to themselves. . . . And to them it is an evil, solely because it corrupts the good of their nature. . . . It is not nature, therefore, but vice, which is contrary to God. For that which is evil is contrary to the good." [2]

It is important to define evil carefully. Augustine's idea that evil is the absence of the good does not seem to be strong enough to express the radical and willful nature that evil demonstrates. But we dare not define evil as whatever displeases us. Determining evil by what displeases us is as bad as determining God and the good by what pleases us. The evil one has an independent nature separate from and prior to our involvement with evil. Just as God determines the good, so the demonic demonstrates evil. Man may interpret both, but man is not the measure of good or evil. When evil or good is determined by man, there is only the subjective idea of what we like or dislike. It is God who determines both good and evil. Good is what God desires. Evil is what God does not desire. These are the best brief definitions of good and evil that I know.

In amplifying this definition of evil I would use the suggestion given in chapter 5. Evil is that which brings death, decay, and fragmentation to God's good creation. Christian theology has affirmed that God permits evil but that he did not directly create it nor will he finally permit it to go unchecked.

Defining evil is difficult, but trying to explain why evil is permitted or what purpose it serves is more difficult still. There is no intellectually or logically satisfying answer to the problem. The three parts of the problem of evil are: God is good; God is all-powerful; yet evil is real. Harsh conclusions could be drawn from these three affirmations. If God is all-powerful, why does he permit evil when he could prevent it? If God is good, how can he allow evil to harm those he loves, especially if he has the power to prevent it?

Some have solved the question of evil by denying one of the parts that make up the problem. Some claim that God is not all-powerful. But the Bible and theological necessity insist that whatever is is because God lets it be. There is an absoluteness in John's statement, "Without him was not any thing made that was made" (John 1:3). God is the source of all power. If he is limited in any way, it is because he has chosen to limit himself. There is a glimpse of truth in the idea that God's power is limited if we can speak of that as a self-limitation. In granting freedom to persons, God has limited himself. But we must acknowledge theoretically that God could remove all self-imposed limitations if he chose to do so.

It is not a solution to the problem of evil to deny that God is good. If God is not good and the standard of goodness, evil itself has no meaning. Unless we equate goodness with God, we place it on a sliding scale of our own convenience. All existence and most of our conversation revolves around some means of making a distinction between what is good, desirable, correct, and right versus what is bad, undesirable, mistaken, and wrong. To remove goodness from the absoluteness of who God is, not only resolves evil, it telescopes good and evil into a paralyzing neutrality.

The third part of the problem of evil has to do with the reality of evil. Is evil real? The Christian Scientist responds that it is not. To deny evil is a naive and impossible position for the human community. The realities of death, decay, and fragmentation bury in their dust all of the finest idealism of the human community. Evil may be defined carefully and may be assigned its limits, but it cannot be denied. We must live with the problem of evil, because we dare not deny any of its parts—God's goodness, God's power, or the grim reality of evil itself.

This simple nursery rhyme is a powerful parable of the fall of man.

As expressed above, the biblical suggestions about the origin of evil involve a threefold possibility. Evil arises from our context, the world. Evil stems from an external force intruding into creation, the demonic. Evil, in a moral sense, is enlarged by our own willful acts, the flesh.

The mystery of the rise of evil and our inability to answer the problem intellectually is complicated by a further question. What, if any, is the purpose of evil? One suggestion is that evil and sin bring justice and punishment to those who do wrong. In many instances this is a correct answer. The glutton who abuses his body must bear the results. But this answer works only in those instances where moral agents have committed immoral acts. The solution of punishment as the answer to evil becomes cruel for the innocent who are destroyed and maimed by a tornado.

A second suggested purpose is that evil makes it possible to learn a lesson from bad consequences. A child who touches a hot stove learns not to do it again. This answer is called the teaching purpose of evil. This answer also fits only a limited number of cases. Experience is a good teacher. Once burned, twice cautious. But what of a body twisted by polio? What of children with cancer? The statement that they can learn to adjust to difficult circumstances is often more harmful than helpful as an answer to their problems.

A third answer as to the purpose of evil is not so much an answer as it is a proposal. This answer says wait and see how things will turn out. You cannot have solutions now, but eventually you will know. This proposal is not to be taken lightly; it is to be taken as a faith expectation. Nevertheless, this does not explain what purpose evil serves. The wait-and-see game is often necessary because it is the only thing we can do. But unless it is accompanied by a lively faith built on past experience, it becomes a thin promise that all will turn out well because we want it to. Certain traumas and forms of intense pain cannot wait. The acute hunger of children and the searing pain of a splintered bone are not helped by a philosophical response that all will work out well. When Christians give the wait-and-see answer to evil, they must accompany it with a diligent attempt to relieve and help the symptoms of what is wrong at the moment.

A more honest answer than those given above is that we

cannot discern that evil serves any purpose. Evil is mysterious and absurd. The open and candid response Christians should make when asked why certain tragedies occur is, "I do not know." Some Christians labor under the mistaken notion that they have to explain evil and give a rational answer to every tragedy. This rests on the false notion that Christians who know God can pry from him secrets not available to others. Christians are not providers of holy secrets; they are witnesses to the open mystery that God has moved to conquer evil in Jesus Christ, his Son. We are not called on so much to explain evil as to embody good. There is, for all persons, an absurd and mysterious element in evil that we cannot understand.

The only answer Christians can provide to the problem of evil is the cross of Jesus Christ. This is God's own cryptic symbol. In his Son, God has taken upon himself evil, suffering, and the consequences of sin. Even evil can become the servant of an ultimate good if there is promise of deliverance from those things that harm. The cross as answer to evil is a practical, definite act that says God is involved with the problem and is not outside it. Persons who suffer could understandably feel hostile toward God if he were outside of their suffering. They could even think God to be the actual cause of it. The cross reminds us that God is with us in our tragedy and that evil is directed at him through us.

It is provocative to realize that since evil cannot attack God directly, it does so through us, his creatures. And in his mercy and sensitivity to us, God has chosen to enter and finally to resolve the problem by his own suffering. The affirmation that God by his suffering helps us in our suffering is called the redemptive answer to evil. This solution leaves many things unanswered, such as why there is evil in the first place. But the redemptive answer is also an answer that gives provisional help. The cross reminds us that we are not alone. It is evidence that God cares for us.

SIN

Evil is that large term for what is wrong with existence. Evil is the opposite of the good. It brings death, decay, and fragmentation. There is a form of evil for which persons are particularily responsible. That is sin. We need not ask why sin happens. We know that we have a part in it. We do need to know what the essence of sin is and what we can do about getting rid of it.

The Christian community has not always been tactful or convincing in telling people what is wrong with them theologically. The preacher who rants about sin is the popular target for movie and TV caricatures. We should take a page from popular psychological insights and reinforce people in their strengths. Our weaknesses are well known to us, and we will feel more like learning about help from those who have taken the time to appreciate and reinforce our strengths. The Christian gospel has much to say about sin, and the Bible always is hardest on those who are most aware of God. A good strategy for speaking of sin is (1) to define it in appropriate ways, (2) to realize that we ourselves are participants in sin, (3) to recognize that the roots of sin are inevitably interwoven with the roots of human achievement.

Defining Sin Appropriately

Describing the debit under which persons live is not easy. In addition to the dilemma posed by the larger category of evil, crisis situations such as death, tragedy, and pain, we must add our own responsible dimensions of sin. Chapters 1, 2, and 4 dealt with what we call original sin. Original sin refers not only to a first sin of a remote ancestor. It also refers to a weakness in all persons which they inevitably exercise by their actual sins. The weakness is a condition of our very existence. The actions of our wills and the misuse of our possibilities is a conscious and intentional process of our own.

PERSONAL LEARNING ACTIVITY 17

In light of the facts you have just studied, read Psalm 51 and Romans 7. List the phrases and terms used to express the plight of persons. Then classify the items on your list. Which speak of a person's weakness and inclination to sin? Which refer to conscious acts of the will?

Sin is well defined in the Bible. Paul spelled out sin as a coming "short of the glory of God" (Rom. 3:23). This implies that sin is an entire posture of life. Sins are specific acts that demonstrate a deeper problem. The problem with equating sin with given cultural do's and don'ts is a serious one. Some people define sin as that which they do not do, or have never wanted to do, or do not have the courage to do. This definition of sin is not adequate for two reasons. (1) Sin is a more pervasive and subtle problem than the listing of a series of acts permitted and acts prohibited. There are things Christians should do and should not do, but these should not be equated with the totality of sin. (2) When we define sin as some few acts, we imagine we can live above them and be rid of sins. If sins were some few actions that we could live above, the price of salvation would not have been as costly as it was. We must not compromise the radical nature of sin by reducing it to a list of do's and don'ts. Sin is falling short of what God is and what he intends us to be. Since sin is assessed by such a large standard, its forgiveness is bought by an enormous price. It is God alone who judges sin. It is the standard he sets that determines sin. The Bible lists many specific sins (Ex. 20 and Gal. 5, for example), but the frame in which sin is painted in the Bible is so large that it can be said, "There is none that does good, no, not one" (Ps. 14:3, RSV). One of our problems in church life today is that we define sin too narrowly. Sin is illustrated by sinful acts, but it is rooted in an essential attitude of life that does not measure up to the fullness of God.

We Ourselves Are Participants in Sin

Abstract definitions of sin are helpful, but the general category *sinfulness* must be illustrated by particular sins. It is popular today to ridicule any particular list of sins. We have helped our youth to resist any specific thou-shall-nots under the criticism that this is a negative religion. The concern in the previous section was to define sin so broadly that people would not identify its essence with violating some cultural rule. The purpose in this section is to spell out those specific attitudes that lead to particular acts of sin. Original sin is the theological term we use for a sinful inclination which we all possess. Actual sin is the individual attitude or deed that makes appropriate the term *sinner*. We are sinful by inclination; we become sinners by act. The difference is in the willful act of sin in which each individual participates.

The criticism has come that the Christian community harps on sin and burdens everyone with false guilt and anxiety. Certain superficial expressions about sin by some Christians have provided fuel for the fire of such criticism. Nevertheless, it is and must be a basic assumption of the Christian faith that there is something wrong with existence and that, in Jesus Christ, God is moving to right what is wrong in his creation. If there is nothing wrong, we do not need God. Jesus said, " 'Those who are well have no need of a physician' " (Matt. 9:12, RSV). He spoke with some sarcasm because he knew that all men need God's help. The beauty of Jesus' expressions about sin is that they were couched in positive terms of grace and forgiveness to those who knew their sins and acknowledged their need of help. His remark in Matthew 9:12 was to religious persons who refused to acknowledge their need of help and forgiveness. There is a powerful lesson for the church in Jesus' posture toward sinners. His teachings about sin should teach us to be more critical of our own lives and less critical of the lives of others. Often we do not demonstrate that we have learned this lesson.

Jesus pointed out specific attitudes and sins wherever he met them and saw their crippling results (Matt. 23). The Bible defines sin in such broad terms that no one escapes the title *sinner*. The Bible also gives many instances where persons are faced with the awareness of their sins in such a way that repentance or destruction are their only choices. The meaning of sin must be understood by the individual and adequately explained by the Christian community so that all understand what is meant by the term *sinner*.

PERSONAL LEARNING ACTIVITY 18

This is a double activity. First, review your work in Personal Learning Activity 16. Note ways you have changed your ideas about the difference between sin and evil. Second, decide what your answer would be to the following question: Can there be any good associated with pride or rebellion or greed or sloth?

The Roots of Sin and Achievement Are Interwoven

Jesus' most provocative statement about sin and righteousness is that the wheat and tares must grow together until they are ready for harvest when they can be discerned readily by their fruits (Matt. 13:24–30). This is an end-time parable, and its primary interpretation is that God, in his judgment, will determine what and who are good and bad. The parable applies to individuals and to nations. It also has a meaning for the reality that good and evil grow simultaneously in the Christian life. What is good and evil is not always so quickly discernible. There are gray areas. We live out of mixed motives.

One of the most demonic and irritating things about sin is that it apes goodness. Sin can be viewed as a relentless wheel on which all persons are caught and tumbled along through life. The essence of sin is fourfold; and no matter how we turn, we are pursued by this built-in debit. Even in our desires to please God, we are plagued by *pride.* When we seek to maintain ourselves, we find it necessary to hold out all others. Holding God out of our lives is the selfish root of *rebellion.* Our legitimate desire to possess, even when it is for the sake of others, often becomes cancerous and enlarges with *greed.* The necessary pause and disengagement from the frantic activity of some church life can and does disintegrate into *sloth.*

Pride.—The positive side of pride is expressed in the biblical idea of glory. The Old Testament word for glory means *weight* or *worth.* To give glory to someone means to recognize his or her worth. To give glory to God is to recognize him as the worthy, weighty person he is. God endowed his creation with its own worth when he declared it good. All of God's creation has its own dignity, because its glory comes from God and its purpose is to give God glory by fulfilling its intended function. When persons recognize the glory of God, they also are recognizing their own worth. Paul called this positive recognition of one's own worth and justifiable pleasure in his or her accomplishments glorying in the Lord (2 Cor. 10:17). The worth of persons comes from the fact that they are made in God's image. Recognizing one's worth and the inherent worth of all others of God's creatures is a legitimate and positive way of being proud.

In its negative aspect pride is raising oneself above others. *Vainglorious* is another term for the negative sense of pride just as *glory* is a positive word for pride. Theologically, pride is trying to play God, thereby displacing him who is God. John Milton asserted that pride is the primal sin. Milton said of Satan, he sought "to set himself in glory above his peers, he trusted to have equal'd the most high." [3] A biblical example of theological pride is the expression of the serpent, "Ye shall be as gods" (Gen. 3:5). Pride, in its negative sense, carries the idea of seeking more than we deserve. Pride could be represented by a directional arrow that points up. When we seek more than we deserve or more than we can use wisely, we are foolish. The adjective *foolish* is often associated with pride, because pride leads people to desire things they cannot or should not attain. The parable of the rich fool (Luke 12:16–20) illustrates the futility of reaching for more than we can possess and desiring to hold it longer than the time granted us to live.

The negative side of pride is bad. The positive side is good. Ironically, they grow together. One who does not have the urge to do, the desire to accomplish, the justifiable pride in his or her good achievements does not offer to God the full glory he deserves. On the other hand, the person who becomes too obsessed with his own achievements becomes vain and arrogant. Political dictatorships in the twentieth century have demonstrated all too clearly the pride of power and its results. Although pride is a root of sin, it also has a positive place in acknowledging the worth and dignity of our accomplishments. If we asked God to cleanse us from all pride, without qualification, it could be a very destructive thing. Pride is a field in which both wheat and tares grow together. We must try, with God's help, to remove as much of destructive pride as we can. But as the new shoots of achievement come up, it is not always easy to distinguish the good from the bad. This ambiguity makes the Christian life a genuine struggle. This ambiguous position is closer both to Scripture and experience than the quick and automatic removal of evil that some proclaim too cheaply.

Rebellion.—The positive side of pride is called *giving God the glory.* The positive side of rebellion is called *striving.* The same physical, psychical, and spiritual energies that are used to rebel can be channeled also in positive ways. The stem of aggression also produces assertiveness. Persistence, striving, resisting in the name of God are all positive human responses of the negative force of rebellion. In some instances rebellion against human authority is a positive thing to do. The early church felt it necessary "to obey God rather than men" (Acts 5:29). The confessing German Church felt obliged to denounce Nazi Germany because of their loyalty to a higher authority.[4] Many minority groups or those who work and live in oppressive social and political circumstances today have drawn the strength of their protest from the New Testament and some of the teachings of Jesus.[5] Old Testament figures such as Abraham and Job contended even with the divine. Jesus' parable of two sons (Luke 15:11–32) strongly suggests that God prefers rebellious sons who repent and do God's will to submissive sons who give him lip service but do not do what the Father asks.

Direct willful rebellion against God always hurts us, because God always wills what is best for us. But there are positive points about resisting any and all things that would overwhelm and stifle our own personhood with its freedom and creativity. The contemporary apostles of a docile and servile submissiveness to those who claim to be God's representatives have confused meekness and weakness. Disciples must be teachable, but they also must be militant for their master. It might be a mistake to ask God to remove from us all aggressiveness and assertiveness, for therein lie the possibilities of fully realizing ourselves for him and by his strength.

The negative aspect of rebellion is a resistance to constituted authority. Theologically, rebellion is a resistance against God. Terms associated with rebellion in the Old Testament are *a willful missing of the mark, treachery, stubbornness, to lean away from.* In the New Testament, willfully missing the mark and rebellion are amplified by such other terms as *strife, disobedience, godlessness, unrighteousness, lawlessness,* and *falling away.*[6]

Rebellion against God and his will often includes violence toward one's fellowmen. A good biblical example of rebellion is Cain's rebellion against God's wish for offerings brought in the proper spirit. Cain's rebellion led to his violence in the murder of Abel.

The old adage "Sticks and stones may break my bones, but words will never hurt me" is not correct. There is psychological and spiritual violence as well as physical violence. In so-called sophisticated circles the violence done to others is often verbal violence. Words can and do hurt terribly. The book of James points out that it is impossible to love and praise God and curse persons at the same time (Jas. 3:9–10).

Montaigne has stated that the essence of our problem is rebellion in the form of disobedience. "The first law that ever God gave to man was a law of pure obedience: it was a commandment naked and simple, wherein man had nothing to inquire after or to dispute, forasmuch as to obey is the proper office of a rational soul, acknowledging a heavenly superior and benefactor. From obedience and submission springs all other virtues, as all sin does from self-opinion." [7]

Direct rebellion against God always has dire consequences. Ordinarily, the Christian will be obedient also to constituted civil authority (Rom. 13). In the instance of oppressive and demonic forms of government, the Christian may have to resist political pressure in the name of God, who is above and over all political structures. Disobedience and rebellion can be seen in every society and at all stages of the life cycle. Rebellion ranges from the willful no of a child to his parents, to the bloody wars of nations, to individual acts of anarchy and terrorism. The directional rebellion points out, holding everyone away from the center of life.

Greed.—Pride can push the self above others and overextend legitimate boundaries. Rebellion can hold all others out and will not acknowledge legitimate boundaries. Greed can pull everything into the self and make one's own desires the boundary of all things. The directional arrow of greed is always pointed in toward the self. The biblical word for greed is *desire.*

Yet, desire can be a positive idea. Paul warned the Corinthians against one kind of desire (covetousness) but encouraged them to another (1 Cor. 5:10–11; 12:31). Zeal is a positive desire. The Bible encourages people to be zealous toward God (Acts 22:3; Titus 2:14). It is possible to be greedy appropriately for God (although that combination of words sounds strange). The difference between good desire and bad desire is the object and our intended use of it. To desire wealth for its own sake or for selfish use is evil. To desire material possessions for those in need or for a worthy cause is good. At times our vision can blur. Our zeal for God can be a way of promoting ourselves. Some forms of dedication have selfish roots.

It would not be wise to ask God to rid us of all desire. The joy of the physical aspect of marriage and the possibility of an adulterous relationship are interwoven. The two-fold possibilities of our desire—desiring good or desiring evil—are an inevitable part of our sinfulness and are also a part of the possibility of victorious Christian living. Those who have painted the struggle as an easy triumph in a mock battle do not understand Paul's statement that he constantly had to struggle with his own desires (1 Cor. 9:27).

In its negative aspect desire is lust or greed. Sinful desire is any appetite that goes out of bounds in what it wants. Adam and Eve desired the forbidden fruit. King David desired Bathsheba, the wife of another. A synonym for a negative desire is *covetousness.* The last of the Ten Commandments forbids coveting those things that another has. Ahab and Jezebel coveted Naboth's vineyard and in their pride committed rebellion and violence to obtain it (1 Kings 21). Jesus forbade covetousness because people's lives are more than their possessions (Luke 12:15). Paul listed covetous persons as especially sinful (1 Cor. 5:10; 6:10). The works of the flesh listed in Galatians 5:19–21 include many that involve greed.

Both covetousness and miserliness are forms of greed. Perhaps the greedy person who merely wants all he can get in order to spend on himself or buy friendships is better than the miser who wants everything he can get in order to keep it for himself. But cupidity (the desire to acquire) and avarice (the desire to hoard) are but two sides of the coin of selfishness. Greed, lust, and covetousness are associated often with sexual sins. Cupidity and avarice are associated with economic sins. All forms of greed want to pull the objects they desire into the center of themselves for purposes of self-gratification. Gluttony is a form of greed. Acquiring friends and treating them like possessions is also a form of greed. A treacherous form of greed is using one's spouse or children as possessions for the gratification of one's own ego. Have you known a father who, in order to satisfy his own ego, pushed his son into athletics? Greed is surely one of the deepest roots of sin.

Sloth.—Pride can push the self up and exceed boundaries. Rebellion can push the self out and deny boundaries. Greed can draw everything into the self and create its own boundaries. Sloth can drag the self down and see no need for boundaries. The directional arrow of sloth points downward like a heavy anchor.

However, the positive pole of sloth is *rest, relaxation,* and *restoration.* The principle of a sabbath rest is essential to men, animals, and machines. To rest perpetually is sloth. To rest intermittently is necessary. All existence seems geared to the tightening and loosening rhythm of the human heartbeat. Without some relaxed pace we would burn out too quickly; we would become dry and brittle and would break.

The idea of furlough for missionaries, of sabbatical leaves for academics, and of vacations for all persons is biologically, psychologically, and theologically sound. Any healthy person must have some time for rest and renewal. The answer to the boredom of our leisure society will not be found in frantic activity. It must be found in creative use of our leisure. Without the positive implications of doing nothing, everything would become hopelessly bland and boringly the same. It would be a mistake to ask God to remove all our possibility of doing nothing, for then life would become one frantic round of endless activity—an existence, as Shakespeare would say, full "of sound and fury, signifying nothing." Persons who stress that Christianity is always doing and never enjoying have not declared the full counsel of God. The danger of sloth comes when we allow the pauses of life to erode its desires for creative performance.

The book of Proverbs is especially hard on sloth. In the wisdom literature sloth is the opposite of diligence. A good synonym for sloth is *laziness* or *lack of concern.* The eighth-century prophets complained against Israel because she did not hear or heed God. The church of Laodicea received severe criticism from the risen Christ because she was neither hot nor cold. The church did nothing (Rev. 3:15). A strong case could be made for the claim that sloth is the most deadly of the sins.[8] Surely sloth is as crippling as any other sin.[9] Other synonyms for sloth are *unconcern, not caring, ignoring,* or *despising the good.* Sloth is the sin of omission. In many ways sloth is the favored sin of religious people who fear punishment for the more active forms of evil.

Summary.—This section on sin has demonstrated that the possibilities of the good and the evil of our existence are interwoven tightly. The wheel of sin has at least four spokes growing out of the midst of the self. We cannot escape, no matter which direction we turn. A composite picture of the wheel of sin would look like this:

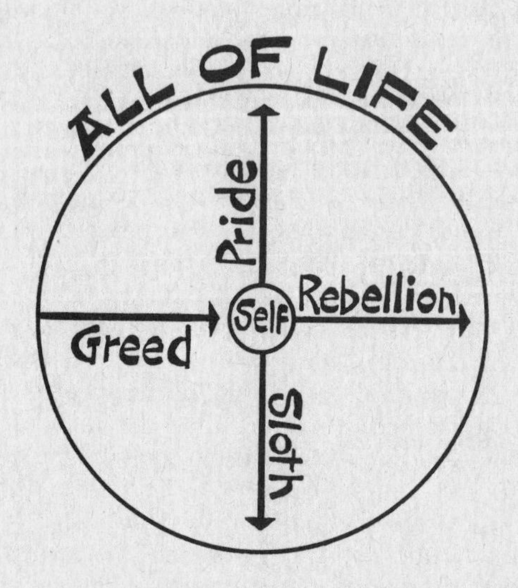

SUMMARY

All of life is rimmed on the spokes that grow from the center of our existence. We are indeed trapped; for if we relax from our pride, we sink into sloth. If we cease holding others out in rebellion, we may gather them in in a greedy, manipulative friendship. Our lives are limited by the evils of death, decay, and pain. They are haunted by the specter of tragedy. Each of us contributes to the store of evil by the individual and willful sins we commit. Groups in our society are no less free from the pride, rebellion, greed, and sloth that motivate individuals. If our story concluded here, we would be fatalists. If our sinfulness were the last word on the subject, we would be pessimists indeed. Evil and sin are essential components of human existence. Without this bad news, there could be no good news. The problem has been diagnosed. It is time to look for solutions. The first step of the solution to the problem of our existence is acceptance—our acceptance by God. This acceptance is the subject of chapter 7.

NOTES

1. *The City of God,* XI, 9.
2. Augustine, *The City of God,* XII, 3.
3. *Paradise Lost,* Book 1, lines 39–40.
4. Compare Karl Barth and Eduard Thurneysen, *Revolutionary Theology in the Making: Barth-Thurneysen Correspondence 1914–1925,* trans. James D. Smart (Atlanta: John Knox Press, 1964).
5. For example, liberation theology (Guiterrez), woman's theology (Rosmary B. Ruether), black theology (James H. Cone).
6. See C. Ryder Smith, *The Bible Doctrine of Sin and of the Ways of God with Sinners* (London: The Epworth Press, 1953).
7. Montaigne's *Essays,* II, 12.
8. See the dialogue among the seven deadly sins in William L. Hendricks, *The Harrowing of Hell* (Nashville: Broadman Press, 1976).
9. Compare Karl Barth, *Church Dogmatics, 1936–69,* Vol. 4, Pt. 2, Sec. 65 (Naperville, Ill.: Alec R. Allenson, Inc., 1969).

Chapter 7
Acceptance

Businessmen speak of the bottom line of a transaction. They mean by this expression how much money a transaction will make or how much a purchase actually will cost. When lawyers use the phrase, they are asking what the legal heart of the issue under discussion is. The taxpayer figures his income, his expenditures, his deductions so that he can get to the bottom line. That is, How much does he owe or how much refund will he receive? It is important to know the bottom line of the Christian gospel. What really is the good news all about?

The good news is about God's acceptance of us in Jesus Christ. That is the essence of the good news, and that is the heart of the gospel. All religious thinking misses the mark when it does not reach this conclusion at the bottom line. The theological term traditionally used to express God's acceptance of us in Jesus Christ is *justification.* This chapter will develop the idea of justification from the perspective of God's taking the initiative, seeking out, and accepting fallen man.

A NEEDLESS SEARCH

A vivid childhood memory of a member of our family involves a fishing trip. The adults who had been fishing discovered that a child was missing. Panic ensued. They began to search frantically. The child who had fallen asleep in an inconspicuous place awakened and silently watched the frantic efforts of her would-be rescuers. Finally, she asked them what they were looking for. With much relief and some irritation, the searchers welcomed the child. She had been there all along. The frenzied actions of the searchers were based on the mistaken notion that the child was lost or drowned and that it was their responsibility to find her. Ironically, the child found them and solved the problem herself.

This incident could be seen as a parable of man's frantic search to rid himself of sin, of his striving for salvation, of his religious quest. The astonishing and ironic message of the gospel, especially expressed by Paul in Romans, is that man's search for salvation and forgiveness is futile. Although both Jews and Gentiles conducted a campaign and search for forgiveness and rightness, they merely complicated the situation further. The God who seemed to them to be lost and had to be won by their deeds and obedience was observing them quietly. He came quietly among them and all of his creation in his Son Jesus Christ. And in Jesus Christ the waiting Father proclaimed to the world that its frantic search was a needless one. The God who is the object of man's desires has never been lost. He has gazed compassionately on the fevered religious efforts of men to discover and to appease a God made in their own image. Grace teaches us that Jesus Christ comes to searching persons who seek forgiveness and release from sin. And as he comes he is the good news that in Christ God accepts us and has forgiven our sins. Our response should be one of great relief and enormous joy. Unfortunately this is not the case.

AN IRRITATING RESCUE

When the adults who sought the lost child were surprised by her presence, their response was one of relief. It was also one of irritation and anger. They were embarrassed because they had not searched thoroughly enough. Their assumptions were wrong. She was not in peril. No dragging of the lake, no calling in areas where she was not, could have accomplished her rescue.

God has not been in peril. He has always stood at the back side of man's religious quest with the quiet news that he has already discovered and redeemed man in the midst of man's needless search for God. God was not lost; the Gentiles were right in recognizing his traces (Rom. 1); the Jews were right in loving his law (Rom. 2); but they took those tokens of God and distorted them into a religious righteousness of their own efforts, which pitched the search in the wrong direction. They took the clues about God and embarked on a futile search for God, based on the mistaken notion that they could find him and earn his acceptance.

The announcement of his acceptance of them declared in the

gospel of Jesus Christ resulted in much irritation. It still does. Romans 1—3 is not talking about the search for salvation and forgiveness of ancient man only. It is also our modern mistake. And we, too, are embarrassed and irritated when God announces from in the midst of us that he has found us and has freely forgiven us.

Grace is God's prerogative, and it is enacted by his sovereign freedom. He has proclaimed the forgiveness of sins and the acceptance of the sinner by virtue of an act that he alone has accomplished. The act whereby persons are forgiven and sin is overcome decisively is the cross of Jesus Christ. Our irritation at this announcement of sheer grace expresses itself several ways.

We Want to Pay Our Way

We are angry because we did not share the cost and satisfactorily make amends for our own sins. It is commendable to pay one's own way in our modern work-oriented-individual-achievement kind of society. The possibility and value of every person's paying his or her own way is often stressed most by people who can least afford it. There is a callous failure in some of us to recognize that many people cannot pay their own way because of handicaps, physical and social disabilities, and lack of opportunity. Social economists rightly argue that it destroys individuality and dignity to do for other people when they should be doing for themselves.

Superficial critics of grace have argued theologically that it is demeaning to man for God to pay the full price of sin, thereby depriving man of working for his own good and striving for his own salvation. This kind of theological response to man's plight seems as unrealistic as the social response of those who suppose that, without help, all people are capable of paying their own way.

When applied to the crucial and pervasive problem of sin, the idea of self-payment becomes absurd. Those who argue that persons should make amends for their own sin have not reckoned with the gravity of the situation. The unanswerable tragedies of human existence must be cared for somewhere. There must be a final court where justice is maintained and effected. Given the inevitable intertwining of the roots of sin with our possibility of goodness, there must be someone to provide for persons who are unable to see their problems adequately or to help themselves.

The Christian gospel declares that it is God who helps people when people cannot help themselves. So long as the possibilities of sin and goodness are grounded in our essential humanity, we cannot separate those actions without destroying ourselves. We must come to God for both diagnosis and cure. It is no shame to seek help when we cannot help ourselves. The first word of the gospel is God's free acceptance of us. It does not destroy our initiative. It provides us with a place to stand where we may work through the second step of the gospel—striving.

Those who are irritated because of the priority of God's acceptance should be aware that their irritation is a part of the effects of the disease of pride itself. We must accept God's acceptance, for it is the only way beyond our impasse. If evil could be resolved by man, and sins and their resultant guilt could be worked out satisfactorily by us, there would be no rational meaning to the cross and no explanation for God's act of sacrifice on our behalf. Man should not be irritated when he discovers that God has granted acceptance and forgiveness in Jesus Christ freely. That is the only solution to our problem. The provision and acceptance of God is our first step before our striving and participating in grace can take place.

We Want to Do Away with the Problem of Sin Itself

Persons confronted by Jesus, who surprises us in our guilt with his declaration of forgiveness, are irritated by the very talk of sin and the need of forgiveness. Augustine was quite correct when he asserted that we cannot rest until we find our rest in God. All men seek God. Many persons disguise this search. They are irritated by it and refuse to recognize the quest for meaning in life as a search for God. They also are extremely distressed because they do not want to acknowledge that sin and guilt, in a variety of forms, do hinder the search for God and meaning in life. This irritation is expressed in two ways. (1) Sin is defined in such ways that it does not become offensive. (2) Persons are asked to forget sin as though it does not exist. These are subtle ways of denying the need of God's acceptance and forgiveness, and the Christian community must answer these challenges.

The redefinition of sin.—Elaborate expressions have been devised to keep from asserting that man is sinner. Chapter 6 freely granted the case that the church often has caricatured sin and has described it in such small, trivial terms that it has seemed a petty thing. But it also suggested that the adequate way to correct that mistake is to define sin in such adequate ways that all would recognize themselves as sinners and that our plight as sinners is inescapable. We cannot redefine sin in other vocabularies to such an extent that it hides the central issue. That central issue is man's estrangement from God who is the ground of our being. There is no objection to treating sin as a sickness or a social malaise. It is not unacceptable to speak of sin as weakness, disability, or a necessary condition of our finitude. Our central objection is that these definitions do not end the need for grace. Sin is sickness, but man and society by themselves do not have its cure. Sin is being finite and needy, but to acknowledge this does not mean that man should consider the sin problem insoluble. God, in grace, has dealt successfully with the dilemma of his creation. Persons who are irritated because they want to decide who we are and what we can do for ourselves describe sin in such a way that God's acceptance is not needed. This is a denial of the gospel.

An attempt to forget sin.—Another way of expressing irritation with God's grace is to suppose that man can overlook sin and forget it. Some psychotherapists, who do not share a religious belief, suggest that the entire discussion of sin and guilt is a debit that Christianity has dropped on Western society. This guilt, so they argue, is a false assumption, for there are no absolutes; and no person is able to tell another that he or she is wrong or unacceptable. The suggestion is ingenious. By denying the premise of sin and guilt, we can remove the problem. There really is nothing wrong with us except our *thinking* that there is something wrong with us.

At first, this sounds like good gospel indeed. Some attempted to forget guilt and deny sin. This has proved to be an ostrich approach to the actual conditions of human existence. Chapter 6 granted that some religious communities have absolutized their own mores and life-styles and called all other customs sin. It also granted that in some Christian communities we have conveyed a false sense of guilt. But when all of this is corrected and made allowance for, it still must be said that there is something desperately wrong with existence that only God can help. God's acceptance of us is no conjured-up condition on which the church capitalizes. It is the indispensable solution to our actual human condition. No one has argued more forcefully for the necessity of recognizing the reality of sin, guilt, and a need of acceptance than Karl Menninger in his book *Whatever Became of Sin?*

In a private discussion, Dr. Menninger asked how I assessed his work. I replied that its basic positions were most welcome and necessary to the Christian community, but that the work did not really satisfy because it does not recognize an ultimate referent for determining sin, namely God.

These irritations with grace—the wanting to pay our own way, the redescription of sin so as to deny the need of grace, the denial of sin and therefore the denial of grace—all are conditions of our clouded vision, which themselves point up the need for God's acceptance.

THE PROCLAMATION OF ACCEPTANCE

We must now turn to the response that is appropriate to an awareness of God's acceptance of us. It is important also to discuss why acceptance is the necessary first step of the Christian message and how it is related to striving, the second pole of the Christian life.

A brief review at this point will help us to see why we must discuss salvation as an integral and necessary part of a book on the Christian view of man. Chapters 1 and 2 portrayed original man as innocent and all persons as interconnected with all others and with the world about them. Chapter 3 elaborated on man's distinctive possibilities in relation to the rest of the created order and in relation to God. Chapter 4 elaborated on man's responsibility and his denial of that responsibility. Chapter 5 stressed that the fall of all persons involved the totality of each person, and chapter 6 spelled out the total effects of evil and sin on God's good creation. A Christian assessment of man can scarcely leave things here. For it is God's intention to secure the goodness of creation, and he is moving to do so in Jesus Christ. That is good news. The first word of the good news is that we, as sinners, are accepted by God. Our awareness of the good news comes through a proclamation of it. Since it is the word of the gospel that brings us to salvation, it is important to define what the gospel is and to note an appropriate response to it.

The Good News of Our Acceptance

We receive different kinds of good news in the mail daily. There is the dubious good news of large give-away prizes for those who buy certain products or invest in land developments. It must be better news to those who actually receive the prizes promised and have the checks delivered.

Another type of good news we receive in writing is letters from friends and loved ones. These words are welcome because they are built on friendship and love. They are received eagerly even when they contain some bad news, for they draw us into a caring relationship that invites our response and a continuing friendship.

There is an ultimate kind of good news. It is the solemn and joyful announcement from God, the ground of our very being, that he has loved us with an everlasting love. He has made us, and he will not cease to be responsible for us. He has moved in Jesus Christ, his Son, to defeat those things that destroy us. He has himself determined to bear the brunt of the suffering produced by evil and the burden of guilt caused by sin. Even in our rebellion, he who created us sustains us in order to redeem us for our own sake and to fulfill his desire for a good creation. This is good news indeed. This is what the world must hear. It is fitting that one New Testament version of our time is popularly called Good News for Modern Man. The basic written source of God's good news for us is found in the Bible. And the kernel of the gospel is found in the proclamation of the early church.

PERSONAL LEARNING ACTIVITY 19

In Acts there are five brief sermons that contain the essence of the good news. Read these sermons and identify the major points of God's good news contained in them. These sermons are found in Acts 2:14–39; 3:12–26; 4:8–12; 5:29–32; 10:34–43.

These words from the earliest disciples are the heart of the gospel and form the basic content of the Christian message. We should learn how these words of proclamation relate to Jesus' sayings and the proclamation of Jesus given by Paul. Then we can draw out the major points of the gospel contained in these sermons.

Jesus, Paul, and Peter

God came looking for us in history, because that is where we live. We were surprised that he appeared among us as he did. All of our search for him, like the parable at the beginning of this chapter, has been concentrated in the wrong direction. While persons of all ages built their Babels (gates to God) toward heaven (the dwelling of God), God himself gently entered history (the arena of men) and announced his good news. Jesus proclaimed that the forgiveness of the Father is available for those who, like the prodigal, will turn to God. Jesus taught that God is the only hope of the dispossessed, the poor, the needy. He further asserted that God alone is judge of all man, and that he judges man's self righteousness to be sin. Jesus taught the kingdom of heaven is a gift and that it is not according to the preconceived mold that we expected. His authoritative teaching asked for a childlike response and a radical obedience to the message of God. Jesus' quiet authority and the drastic surprise of the appearance of God in our history in that way occasioned the irritation toward grace, discussed above. In Jesus' own day this irritation became so intense that it caused his death. Ironically, his death and resurrection were the final evidences of his proclamation of a gospel of grace. The cross and the resurrection became the acted-out event of the good news that God himself was bearing the cost of evil and sin.

Paul perceived that Jesus' cross and resurrection were the seals of his testimony about God's grace. Paul became the first proponent, in writing, of this radical concept of God's gracious acceptance. It was a dramatic conversion indeed for Saul of Tarsus to realize that man's quest for God's approval was the wrong way to search for God. Paul was overwhelmed by the reality that God had come into history and had already effected his salvation and acceptance of man. Paul's gospel was his own (Gal. 1). His conversion was the gift of God (Acts 9:1–8). Nevertheless, Paul shared with the early church a common gospel about the meaning of who Jesus was and what his death and resurrection meant. Jesus was God's gospel. Paul's is the first written witness to that gospel. He gave an accurate interpretation and application of the gospel embodied in Christ. This we may indeed call "the sure word of the gospel." The good news of God's acceptance of us is called the *kerygma,* and it contains four basic points.

The Kerygma, the Content of the Good News

The Greek word we transliterate as *kerygma* means the content of a message proclaimed by a herald. We translate the word in English as *preaching.* Unfortunately, Paul's frequent use of the term *preaching* in 1 Corinthians 1 has been assumed by some to mean that the act of preaching is the instrument of our salvation. This passage should be translated so that it is clear that it is not the act of preaching but the content of what is preached—the gospel—that is the saving instrument of God.[1] God grants grace to his creation and freely accepts men in their sins. This acceptance is proclaimed by persons, but the basis for this acceptance is the act of God in Jesus Christ. The message that speaks of this acceptance is the *kerygma,* the content of the good news. The good news has five essential points.

Christ came from God.—It was not easy for the earliest believers to recognize or accept that Jesus had come from the God of Abraham, Isaac, and Jacob. Paul's greatest dilemma must have been in believing that the Messiah he had looked for had already come and had been crucified by those who were most expecting him (see especially Gal. and Rom. 9—11). The *kerygma* is the first Christian confession that Jesus is Lord. This is a full acknowledgment that Jesus has come from God and shares God's own nature. To call Jesus Christ "Lord" is to recognize that he is the clearest picture of God the world has and that he is an extension of God himself to us. The beauty of the idea is that Jesus not only brings the word of God to us; he is uniquely the word of God for us. The proclaimer of God has rightly become the proclaimed one about what God has done for us.

His death was caused by sinful persons.—Jesus foresaw the irony of his predicament in the parable of the unjust stewards whose rebellion against the master extended even to the death of his only son (Mark 12:1–11). In Acts Peter boldly charged the Jews of his day with the death of Jesus. The involvement of Pilate and the total political structure of Rome cannot be denied a place in the crucifixion. Paul broadened the scope to see the logical connection that since all persons sin, all participate in the crucifixion of Christ. It was a cosmic event in which the innocent assumed the place of the guilty and became their representative as well as God's representative. The vertical of the divine representative and the horizontal of human representation intersect as the meeting place of God and his creation.

God raises him up.—The miraculous act of God in overcoming evil and sin is the resurrection of Christ. By this absolute and unique event God gives to all his creation the promise of life in spite of death. A Christian discussion of mankind cannot omit the epochal event of resurrection which speaks of the ultimate destiny of persons and of God's good intent for them. Resurrection is not a wakening from sleep or a mere resuscitation of a body to live life under the continuation of earthly existence. Resurrection is a whole new kind of life that brings God's own dimension and type of life to his creation. Resurrection is God's own free gift, and it is his own doing. It is the hallmark of his acceptance of us. The resurrection of Christ is an indispensable part of the proclamation to man about God's acceptance.

Jesus sends the Spirit.—Just as God sent Jesus, so Jesus sends the Spirit. The act of God in accepting us is threefold. The Father sends the Son; the Son glorifies the Father and sends the Spirit; the Spirit bears witness to the Son and extends the presence of the Father to his creation. This threefold rhythm of God's action in accepting us makes necessary the Christian idea of the trinity or the threefoldness of God. *Trinity* is not a biblical word, yet some concept of God as threefold is the only possible conclusion we can reach when we observe the full movement of God in our direction.

God began and will conclude his creation.—The words of the earliest Christian *kerygma* include an awareness that God who began the world will also conclude it. Involved in the last act of God is the twofold sequence of the sending of the Spirit, who is the down payment of his ultimate presence, and the sending of his Son to judge all men (Acts 10:42). The implication is that judgment is gracious and intended to be redemptive (Acts 3:26). The conditions for God's judgment through Christ are expressed. They are *repentance* and *faith* in relation to Christ. These conditons are the necesary response of man to the free promise of God's acceptance.

PERSONAL LEARNING ACTIVITY 20
Without looking back, recall the five essential points in the kerygma. Then look back and check your recall.

AN APPROPRIATE RESPONSE TO GOD'S ACCEPTANCE

This chapter has spoken thus far about God's acceptance of us. This is the first word of the gospel. However, a direct address anticipates a response. An invitation seeks an answer. God's grace is free and his acceptance is complete. But neither his grace nor his acceptance of persons is unconditional. God's acceptance invites our appropriate response.

What is an appropriate response to the news that we have been healed and redeemed from an unexpected quarter while we strove to do it for ourselves? The parable at the beginning of this chapter supplies the answer. When the searched-for comes up behind the searchers and calls into question all of their searching, he should be met with great joy and deep relief. There should be celebration at the discovery. Certainly this is the gracious attitude of God expressed in the character of the waiting father in Luke 15:11–32. The response of the prodigal son in that same parable is a model of how persons should respond to the good news of God's free acceptance. Our first response is a coming to ourselves. We call this repentance. Repentance is also a determination, with God's help, to turn to him.

The indispensable element from our part in having God's free acceptance is to accept it. This acceptance of our acceptance by God is called faith. It is illustrated by the return of the prodigal, who, aware of his problem, nevertheless believed that his father would receive him. The only adequate response to the overwhelming acceptance of God's free grace is to say fervently, "Thank you, I'll take it."

The delight of finding Jesus safely on our shore after our frantic search for God elsewhere and our determined efforts to fend for ourselves is expressed in the story of the disciples returning to find the resurrected Christ after a fruitless night of fishing (John 21:1–13).

To experience the acceptance of God we must respond with repentance and faith. The path for man's becoming what he was intended to be begins with these two steps, repentance and faith.

Repentance

The term *repentance* is not always palatable to modern tastes. For some it conjures up emotional excesses and groveling before God. Repentance in the Bible is associated only rarely with these ideas. Repentance is a decided act of the mind and will as much as of the emotions. Repentance involves a deliberate and intentional turning around and a change of mind. It expresses a desire to have things be different from what they were. We must not squelch any root of genuine repentance, for repentance comes in a variety of shapes and may be expressed in any number of ways. What is to be avoided is any idea of repentance that is not genuine and does not involve the totality of a person, including the person's actions as well as his emotions. I like Luke's impression about the prodigal son as an adequate model of repentance. Repentance is a "coming to ourselves" when we hear the word of God's acceptance. Our response is a homecoming to the Father God who made us and appeals to his fragmented image within us. The keynote of repentance is not a mournful sorrow. The keynote of repentance is joy.

Faith

The second act of man that is necessary to receive the acceptance of God is *faith.*[2] The primary meaning of faith is to assert a thing is true. The religious word *amen* comes from the Old Testament word for truth. To say amen to a thing is to declare that it is true, to believe in it. Paul asserts that all of the promises of God are given a solemn amen in Jesus Christ (2. Cor. 1:20). To accept Jesus Christ as God's instrument of his acceptance of us is to say amen to God's acceptance of us. It is the yes all creation utters to the Creator, or would if man's distortions did not prevent it. (Man alone was given the power to negate his responsibility of affirming God.) Tragically, mankind by its distortion of the remainder of the created order, often has prevented the full yes which other creatures are expected to give to God.

Willfully to say no to God's acceptance of us in Christ has damning and awesome consequences. It is this no of the creatures of God that has created the problem of sin and evil in existence. It is the opposite yes of affirmation that the rebellious creature must bring in order to know the acceptance of God. The responsibility is once more upon us. Yet we cannot assert that our answer is totally within our own power. The Bible reminds us that we are also enabled by God to respond to him. Ephesians 2:8–9 points up the priority of God in both granting us acceptance and in aiding us in our acceptance by giving us the gift of faith.

Just as repentance has been distorted to suggest emotional excess, faith has been called blind belief in the face of all evidence to the contrary. Faith is not basically a contrasting opposite to reason. John Dillenberger has said wisely that genuine faith does not outrage reason; rather it outruns it.[3] Faith is based on an object that lies beyond the senses' perceptions. That object is God. But this object of faith resonates with man's desires and his keenest inclinations and aspirations toward fulfillment and meaning. There is enough historical element in the Bible and Christian tradition to keep faith from being blind. But there is also enough mystery and transcendent promise in the Bible to keep faith geared toward that which cannot be seen.

As usual, the answer to the criticism of a distorted view of faith is an adequate perspective of faith. Full biblical faith involves the head of men, which includes his thinking ability to respond to the gospel. It involves the heart of man, which, in modern ways of speaking, includes the emotional and motivating elements of the individual. Full biblical faith also involves the will of the individual whose faith is a doing as well as an accepting and a believing.[4]

SUMMARY

Just as persons are totally affected by sin, so are they totally involved in faith. This chapter has stressed the first word of the gospel, which is acceptance or justification. God's acceptance of us precedes and is the basis of our ability to accept him. The only condition to our receiving God's acceptance is our acceptance of it. That acceptance involves our repentance and faith. Even these are dispositions God gives. He has come to us in ways we did not expect, and we are startled by the discovery of what we searched for so vainly by ourselves. It is grace. Let us not be irritated. Let us rejoice and celebrate that God has found us, even as he rejoices when, by his grace, we find ourselves and come home.

NOTES

1. Gerhard Kittel (ed.), *Theological Dictionary of the New Testament* (Grand Rapids: Wm. B. Eerdmans Publishing Co., 1968).

2. For biblical studies on faith and repentance, see J. J. Von Allmen, *A Companion to the Bible* (New York: Oxford University Press, 1958); Alan Richardson, *A Theological Wordbook of the Bible* (New York: The Macmillan Co., 1951); and Kittel, *ibid.*

3. John Dillenberger, *Faith, a Handbook of Christian Theology,* ed. Marvin Halverson (New York: World Publishing Co., 1969), pp. 128–32.

4. See Rudolf Schnackenburg, *Belief in the New Testament* (New York: Paulist Press, 1974). Note that doctrinal, motivational, and ethical ideas are all bound up with faith. It is to be remembered that all subsequent faith is built on the faith of the first believers, the apostles. There is an element of heritage as well as of immediacy to faith.

Chapter 8
Striving

At a church picnic in my early teenage years I chose to freeze the ice cream while all the others played games and enjoyed themselves. Those were the days of wooden buckets and hand-turned cranks. It was an arduous task, and my arm grew weary. Finally, one of the sponsors noticed my heroic deeds. She asked what I was doing. I replied that I had been working while others played, and the ice cream was nearly frozen. She then informed me that the ice cream mix was on the table and that my "nearly frozen ice cream" was an empty cylinder of very cold air. It is a tale many Christians could recognize. All our striving, even for God, unless done in the proper spirit and unless filled with the Spirit produces a vacuum of very cold air.

The Christian life has been described by Paul as a walk. He was not speaking of taking a walk merely for leisure or for recreation. The Christian walk is a way of life; and as a way of life, it involves motion. Life itself involves motion and mobility. Perhaps the best known Christian classic in English which describes the Christian life as a journey is John Bunyan's famous *The Pilgrim's Progress.*[1]

Life is a journey, and life involves striving. The Christian life is no exception. It is important that the Christian walk and the Christian journey begin with the right foot forward. Like every walk, the Christian journey is made with both feet. The two feet on which Christian life moves through the journey of life are acceptance and striving. It is crucial that the first step be acceptance (traditionally called justification). The second step must be striving (traditionally called sanctification). After serious illness and surgery, people sometimes have to learn to walk again. The new birth brings us into a different rhythm of life where we too must learn to walk properly. And the proper walk of a Christian is first an awareness of our acceptance and then a striving to live out of that acceptance. In this chapter there are three topics we must touch: (1) Why acceptance before striving? (2) The dimensions of striving—its goal and its rhythm. (3) We do not strive alone.

WHY ACCEPTANCE BEFORE STRIVING?

Acceptance is the first and basic step of the Christian experience. Emphasizing this fact is important. This is not merely quibbling about how to start things. The rhythm of the whole walk of a Christian person needs to stress the priority of grace and the initiative of God's acceptance. It is necessary to explore the unsatisfactory patterns of a religious walk so that we can explore what all of this attention to priority is about. Patterns other than the acceptance-striving pattern are striving for acceptance, acceptance to the extent of striving, and acceptance only.

Striving for acceptance denies grace.—The pattern of striving for God's acceptance is a denial of grace. Paul's pre-Christian experience is a classical case. His experience embodies the frustration and failure of all legalist forms of religion. Man is indeed incurably religious. The sad story of persons' attempts to appease the gods and buy salvation is apparent in the study of all world religions. J. S. Whale has set forth accurately the steps of a legal religion that sees sacrifice as a way of buying divine favor. (1) The first stage is that of crude bargaining, the offerings of a gift or a sacrifice. (2) The second stage is the moralistic stage. This moves beyond sacrifice to an ethical endeavor. (3) The third stage is utter self-abasement in the realization that one's best is still unworthy before God.[2]

Chapter 6 showed that sin is too subtle and all pervasive for any person to escape. The parable in chapter 7 about the lost child who finds her seekers is a parable of grace. It is really true that our condition is such that only God can help us. And it is equally true that God has chosen to help us by his unexpected and undeserved act of grace in Jesus Christ on our behalf. Striving to attain salvation is not unappreciated. It is simply impossible. Striving to gain acceptance is flattering to our ego, but it is devastating in its outcome. It is devastating because the requirements and intentions of God for his creation are so high that he alone can meet them. And it is devastating because sin is so radical that it blurs our vision of what is right and distorts the possibility of our doing what is best for us without God's help.

Striving to gain acceptance is self-defeating. It is not God's way of grasping man. Nor is it a possible way in which man can grasp God. We feel that we ought to have made things right in God's fractured creation, for we helped to make them wrong. The truth is that we cannot make them right. But he has done so in Jesus Christ. He has accepted the unacceptable, even in their vain striving to find him. The acceptance of his grace brings salvation. The rejection of his acceptance brings lostness and the continued frustration of striving on our own to do the impossible—lift ourselves by our own bootstraps. The confusion of Babel (Gen. 11) is the inevitable result of all legalist forms of religion that promote striving to be accepted.

Acceptance to the extent of striving creates insecurity.—There is a more subtle, unsatisfactory alternative to the acceptance-striving pattern of the Christian walk. It is the pattern of being accepted to the extent to which one strives. This accepted-to-the-extent-of-striving pattern differs from the crucial point of recognizing that God's acceptance must precede man's striving. This second pattern at least acknowledges the priority of grace. It proclaims that we are saved by grace but immediately transfers us to a basis of works in order to feel accepted. Its greatest weakness is its failure to continue the Christian walk as it has begun it. Our acceptance by God is a continuing acceptance. Christian existence always swings out first with the bold assurance of God's acceptance, followed by the striving of the person aided by God.

Two weaknesses of the view that we are accepted only to the extent that we strive are (1) the lack of assurance about our acceptance by God and (2) the possibility that we will become unacceptable to God again because we are not striving enough.

The loss of assurance of God's acceptance is a severe blow. The child who is uncertain of his father's acceptance is often deeply troubled about how he should act and is deeply insecure. God's acceptance of us is true because of his affirmation that he has accepted us. Our acceptance by God is not dependent on our feelings of acceptance. Disobedience and lack of striving can drive wedges between us and God. But the way to start again in the Christian walk is with the first step of confidence that we can always move anew out of a sense of that acceptance.

Acceptance without striving disclaims responsibility.—One further unsatisfactory alternative to the acceptance-striving model of the Christian walk should be noted. It is the supposition that the acceptance of God is all that persons need and that there is no need for people to strive once they have been and continue to be aware of their acceptance. The fallacy of this acceptance-only view may be demonstrated by use of our metaphor of walking. Those who insist on acceptance only seek to avoid all responsibility are like persons trying to walk with only one leg. They are immobile for they are not able to swing forward on the second foot and progress in their walking. Both acceptance and striving are required. It is a matter of seeing that the right step comes first. Paul's response to those who seek to walk only on the leg of acceptance is: "What shall we say then? Shall we continue in sin, that grace may abound? God forbid" (Rom. 6:1–2). The Creator-Redeemer God holds both lost and saved persons as responsible. The good news of the gospel is God's acceptance, and the full meaning of the gospel involves our striving.

PERSONAL LEARNING ACTIVITY 21
Think about the three unsatisfactory alternatives to the pattern of acceptance and striving in the Christian life. As you consider each one, identify times in your life when you may have been following that alternative. What factors contributed to your doing so? What factors contributed to your return to acceptance-striving as the pattern for your life?

By examining the unsatisfactory alternative patterns to the acceptance-striving way of walking in Christian existence, we have answered the original question about why acceptance should be the first step of the gospel and striving the second. To strive for acceptance is to try to walk backward. It is ineffective because we are not made that way. To suppose we are accepted only to the extent that we strive is to be paralyzed into the shuffling immobility of doubting God's acceptance, or supposing that we can lose it. Only by stepping first with God's acceptance followed inevitably by the second step of our striving may we successfully and naturally walk the Christian way. A Christian view of man must stress this necessary sequence of justification and sanctification as the way in which persons begin to walk toward their fulfillment in God.

THE DIMENSIONS OF STRIVING

I have translated the biblical word *justification* as acceptance and the biblical term *sanctification* as striving. Striving is a person's being set apart to God and that person's gradually becoming like the God to whom he or she is set apart. This implies a goal to our striving. There is also a rhythm to our striving. The gradual becoming like God acknowledges advances and setbacks, both gains and losses. Paul captured the idea of the rhythm in Christian striving when he said: "I know what it is to be brought low, and I know what it is to have plenty. I have been very thoroughly initiated into the human lot with all its ups and downs—fullness and hunger, plenty and want" (Phil. 4:12, NEB). [3] It is my view that a goal out before man and the rhythm of ups and downs is common to the basic composition of mankind. The goal and pattern are inherent in us as humans. The God who made us has planted the goal and the urge for striving within us, and he himself will provide the fulfillment and possibility for attaining them. Each of these dimensions of striving deserves a separate look.

The Goal

The idea of a goal has intrigued persons since the beginning of our records about human behavior. People have always wanted to know what lies beyond their mountains. This insatiable curiosity has led to magnificent achievements and overwhelming failures. Whatever the result, the impulse cannot be denied. In Lisbon, Portugal, there is a magnificent statue to the navigators and explorers who set out from that country to explore the world that lay beyond their shores. Portugal still considers the age of the explorers as her golden age. I once saw a great number of people in the new museum of space and aircraft in Washington, D.C. Nearly all were intrigued. However, while the older generation was reveling in Charles Lindberg's *Spirit of St. Louis,* their children were fascinated with the *Apollo* capsules. Both gave evidence of the lure of goals and their achievements. Our spectator sports-conscious age has bases and baskets and goal posts. All of them speak of a desired end, of something to be accomplished. Without goals, meaningful life ceases. When people lose the desire to eat, to move about, to achieve, life deteriorates. Most of our daily goals are set for us by the routine expectations of our jobs and our daily schedules. When these are removed, it is often a traumatic or troubled time.

Browning expressed in poetic form the need for goals. "A man's reach should exceed his grasp, or what's a heaven for?" That is truly a profound insight. The very notions of God and heaven are bound up with that seeking quality that God has planted in us. It is helpful to remember Augustine's insight about the restless heart. "Thou madest us for Thyself, and our heart is restless, until it repose in Thee." There is something of God in all of the worthy goals of men. There is also the tendency of goals that are geared in the wrong direction to become tools of the demonic. The idea that goal striving is both good and bad is further corroboration that the roots of our sinfulness and our sanctity are interwoven.

One of the major problems of our affluent society is the loss of goals or the too-easy attainment of our material goals. The result is a crippling boredom that smothers our creativity. Every elementary school teacher knows the necessity of keeping pupils aware of a learning experience that will provide adequate motivation for learning. There is a dilemma of boredom in the church when people are given limited vision and goals. Paul's expression about his own striving is well translated in *The New English Bible.* "For my part, I run with a clear goal before me; I am like a boxer who does not beat the air; I bruise my own body and make it know its master, for fear that after preaching to others I should find myself rejected" (1 Cor. 9:26–27, NEB). Another classic expression of Paul about goals and motivation is: "My friends, I do not reckon [consider] myself to have got hold of it yet. All I can say is this: forgetting what is behind me, and reaching out for that which lies ahead, I press towards the goal to win the prize which is God's call to the life above, in Christ Jesus" (Phil. 3:13–14, NEB). The early apostle of Christianity had no time for boredom because his goal was set high enough to lead on toward an exciting and fulfilling life.

Cervantes' Don Quixote is an intriguing figure. He has grasped the imagination of our day through the modern musical version of *Man of La Mancha.* Don Quixote is a character who often selects the wrong goals, who mistakes minor goals as major battles. Even in incredible instances, he believes the best about people and insists on the tension of the ideal. In this comic character there is something reminiscent of the Christian vision and suggestion of the Christian goal. It is important also for Christians to learn to dream the impossible dream.

God gives his creation a goal. He is himself the goal. To be without goals is to be without life. To be without an ultimate goal is to be without God. Striving is a necessary step in life. It is the necessary secondary word of the gospel. Striving, the motion of life, comes quickly after acceptance, the gift of God's new life to us.

The Rhythm of Striving

If the song "The Impossible Dream," from the musical version of *Man of La Mancha*, expresses our need for a goal, the refrain of the spiritual "Nobody Knows the Trouble I've Seen" expresses the rhythm of striving. The words that most accurately express the rhythm is "I'm sometimes up and sometimes down." That which never meets resistance gains no strength. It is no adequate explanation to say that evil and sin are permitted in order to build character and to provide moral muscle. But it is appropriate in our struggle with evil and sin.

Just as we saw a divine intention in the inherent goals of all life, we may see a purpose in the ups and downs of the rhythm of striving. This rhythm is true in creation as well as in redemption. It is demonstrable in the world of nature as well as in the realm of people. It would seem that the desired result would be to have all ups and no downs, all easiness and no hard times. But it does not work out that way. Overfed and overwatered crops or houseplants are prey to rot, mildew, insect blight, or dying from rigorous weather. We speak of all creatures having natural enemies. Modern biological studies have seen in this general law an important balance of nature. Current ecological studies point up the dilemma we face because of man's desire to remove all downs and to dictate life solely for his own comfort. Modern medicine has pointed out to us that the increased pressures of an always up society have brought on a killing onslaught of stress diseases. Mankind is unwise always to be seeking only ups, only successes, only more. The previous section alluded to the danger of boredom in an affluent society. Edward Gibbon's *The Decline and Fall of the Roman Empire* provides many interesting parallels for our own society. There are destructive problems of injustice and morality that arise in an affluent culture such as our own. The old adage "Those who do not learn from history are doomed to repeat it" is appropriate for our time. It is bad for the rhythm of a striving life always to be up or successful without meeting resistance. The stress of always being successful comes in the enlarged fear of failure; the danger in always being successful comes in the problem of boredom.

These stresses and dangers are also implicit in Christian striving. The Christian who thinks he has learned to live above temptation, sin, and the possibility of failure is sinful. He is sinful because he has not adequately reckoned with the pervasiveness and radicality of sin. He is sinful because he has fallen into pride and self-righteousness. He is sinful and vulnerable because he has not adequately counted on the cunning of the evil one. He is especially sinful because he lacks sympathy and compassion for those whose lives are fragmented and broken by sin. Always being up sounds like an ideal rhythm in striving. It is not. It is not ideal because it overlooks the reality of who we are in the midst of a troubled existence, where even the trouble can contribute to our strength. Evil requires good to define it. Down requires up to define it. The reverse is not necessarily true, or else evil and down would be eternal, and they are not.

It should not be necessary to spend much time arguing that always down is not an adequate rhythm of striving. The problems associated with success are stress and boredom. Those associated with constant failure are deprivation and despair. The runt of the litter often is deprived of necessary nourishment. The stunted tree in a heavily wooded spot never receives its share of sunlight. The person who is down physically, mentally, and spiritually is deprived, and it is a desperate situation. The person who is down physically we call ill. The person who is down mentally we call depressed. The person who is permanently down spiritually we call unsaved. *Lost* is a good word to describe all three of these conditions. In the physical realm, one has lost his health; in the mental realm, one has lost his equilibrium; and in the spiritual realm, one has lost sight of God. Hell is to be deprived. Chapter 9 will connect the ideas of evil as a lacking and lostness as deprivation.

The second characteristic of an always down rhythm of striving is despair. One of the most poignant passages about despair in recent literature is found in Alex Haley's *Roots*.[4] Kunta Kinte descends into the despair of slavery after his capture in Africa. Every new experience brings an overwhelming awareness that there is no hope for things to be as they once were. His brutal capture, the slave ship, the maiming of his body, and finally the loss of his spirit to fight back are all steps in a tale of overwhelming discouragement.

The rhythm of Christian striving must include some discouragement. John reminds us that "the whole world is in the power of the evil one" (1 John 5:19, RSV). Modern Christians should expect to face all of the honest dilemmas the earliest Christians knew. Our hymnody is enriched by the titles that reflect the despair that occasionally comes with the struggles and the downs of Christian existence. "Must Jesus Bear the Cross Alone," "Jesus, I My Cross Have Taken," "No, Not Despairingly" share something of an awareness that the down of despair is one part of the rhythm of Christian striving.

Paul was a man of balanced and rich experience. From his epistles we read a reflection of our own experience. "Hard-pressed on every side, we are never hemmed in; bewildered, we are never at our wits' end; hunted, we are never abandoned to our fate; struck down, we are not left to die" (2 Cor. 4:8, NEB).

WE DO NOT STRIVE ALONE

Acceptance as God's justifying gift of life precedes striving, which is our movement in the life God gives. Striving necessarily involves the idea of a goal and inevitably involves a rhythm of up and down. The next questions are crucial. Do we strive alone? Is the striving of existence a lonely, heroic act of man? Or are there resources from beyond himself in the striving of life?

This is a book about the Christian doctrine of man. Most of its affirmations could be supported also by secular means. It can be established by the biological and social sciences that persons have common needs and share a basic human heritage. The descriptions of humanity given in chapter 3 were drawn not only from the Bible but also from the encyclopedia. The idea that man seeks to transcend the self—expressed in the religious term, the image of God—has been recognized also in humanist and psychological studies. The plight of persons because of evil, finitude, and sinfulness is the subject of both the fine arts and the television soap operas. Christianity has no monopoly on describing the miseries of mankind. Even the previous section of this chapter applies to life in general. Striving toward goals in an up and down rhythm is a part of all life. Only in chapter 6 and in this section of chapter 8 do we bring an exclusively Christian message about people. God's acceptance of us in Jesus Christ is universal good news. But it is news that all people do not know. Striving in life is the lot of all people. But the knowledge that we do not strive alone is a distinctively Christian part of the good news of the gospel. Christianity has three pieces of good news to share. (1) Through Christ, God has accepted us freely (chap. 6). (2) Through Jesus Christ and the Holy Spirit, God gladly helps us (this section of chap. 8). (3) In the end God will perfect us (chap. 9).

It is the presupposition of the Bible that grace is built on nature, that God the Redeemer is also the Creator. It is also a presupposition of the Bible that he who made the world has not abandoned it. It is the good news of grace that he is moving to redeem his creation. This movement of redemption is historically effected by Jesus Christ, and it is subsequently applied by the Holy Spirit. The Christian is possessed by the delightful secret that must be shared. We do not strive alone. Neither nature nor grace is a lonely state.

It is a basic belief of the Christian community that God upholds the world. This is not to be understood physically—like Atlas, the giant who holds the world on his shoulders. God's guiding presence in his creation may be seen best by the eyes of faith, which look beyond all secondary effects to God who is the first cause of all things. We cannot prove God exists by the design of the world or by the marvelous structure of the universe—if by prove one means mathematical and physical certainty. But we can establish with great probability that the very structure of our world points to an infinite intelligence that lies beyond our world and brought it into being. It is by the historical revelation of the Bible and the corresponding experience with a caring God that we can assert that a personal, loving God upholds the world he created. Christians call this upholding care God's providence. A good theological definition of providence is: providence is God's guiding the world he made to the good he desires by the means he chooses.[5] Biblical expressions of

God's providence are found in Job 37—41 and especially in Jesus' teachings in the Sermon on the Mount (Matt. 5—7). A modern melodic expression of providence is given in the spiritual "His Eye Is on the Sparrow." All of these expressions add up to the assertion that God has not left his creation alone. He strives with it and for it and in the midst of it.

God is present with his creation even when mankind distorts and disallows his presence (Rom. 1:19–21). It is reassuring to know that God strives with all of his creation, leading it toward its fulfillment. It is an intimate and personal promise of the Christian message that those who accept God's acceptance are bolstered also by the special grace of his strength in their individual striving. Christians do not strive alone. They strive in the strength of God through the person of Jesus Christ and in the power of the Holy Spirit.

Striving with Christ

The old spiritual "Jesus Walked This Lonesome Valley" says that nobody else could walk it with him; he had to walk it by himself. And that verse is correct. He was a man of sorrows and acquainted with grief. But the next verse of the spiritual lacks the promise of the gospel. The second verse asserts that we must walk our lonesome valleys, and no one else can walk them for us. In the sense that each person must be himself and fulfill his own destiny, that is true. But there is a greater truth that the second verse of the spiritual omits. Since Jesus has walked his lonely valley, he bore that ultimate loneliness so that we would not have to. Because he walks with us, we do not bear an ultimate loneliness.

The Christian should not view his life as a heroic attempt to establish his individuality against the gods and all other competing forces. Christians do not have to compete with Jesus. They need to be helped by him. The first and indispensable help that Jesus brings us is the word that by his sacrifice God accepts us and is moving to make things right. Jesus' first call is for us to stop searching and striving for God's acceptance in places where we cannot find God and in ways which cannot buy his favor. When Christ has found us with his first word of acceptance and forgiveness, he then continues with us in a celebration of presence and a strengthening of the inner man. The Christ who strives with us is the Jesus of Nazareth who died for us. His first help is to secure and announce our forgiveness. His second help is to provide a model for our striving and to give us the support of a friend at court. A Christian vocabulary would call these helping tasks of Christ the tasks of Prophet, King, and Priest. As the proclaimer of our salvation, Christ is Prophet. As the one who gives the decree of eternal life and ultimate acceptance, he is King. As the one who continues to intercede for us and to represent us before God, he is Priest.

It will lead to a one-sided distortion if we try to make too fine a distinction between the helps Christ gives us. It is better to say that God has supplied all our needs in Christ Jesus (Phil. 4:19). In Jesus Christ, God has fulfilled the classical prayer "Demand what you will, O God, but give what you demand." In Jesus Christ, God has done something for us we cannot do for ourselves. He has provided free acceptance. He has given us a sense of love and worth. And he has begun to overcome all of those things that threaten us. It is really good news that Jesus Christ is with us in the striving of life.

Striving in the Spirit

Another gracious gift Christ gives us is the extension of himself in the power of the Holy Spirit. In the writings of John, the teaching about Christ's gift of the Holy Spirit to strive with us is especially pertinent. John taught especially that God sent the Son. The Son came to destroy the works of the evil one. The Son finished his work in history, and his presence was removed from men. It was necessary that the physical presence of the Son should go away so that the universal presence of the Holy Spirit could come. When the Holy Spirit comes, he extends the presence of Christ. He bears witness to the Son, and he acts as another witness to God and brings the presence of God. The presence of the Holy Spirit with the Christian is a grace gift that guides the Christian into all truth, that convicts the Christian of all sin, and that comforts the Christian in all afflictions. As Jesus is our help at God's court (Heb. 4:14–16; 7:25–28), the Spirit is our help from God's court (John 14:15–18; Rom. 8:26–27). [6]

Paul's way of talking about the help the Spirit gives Christians in their striving complements John's perspective. In Paul's thinking the Spirit is God's pledge or down payment of the final presence of God himself. It is by the enabling power of the Holy Spirit that persons are able to recognize and confess Christ as Lord. Man's spirit interprets man's own innermost self and God's spirit interprets the deep things of God. It is the Holy Spirit who makes possible Christian life, because he opens our lives to the gospel. It is the Holy Spirit also who makes possible our continuation of the Christian life by granting gifts to the body of Christ through individual believers. These gifts are to be used to build up the entire body of Christ and to produce the fruits of the Spirit which give evidence of Christian growth. [7] These brief descriptions illustrate a wealth of biblical insights designed to assure us that we do not strive alone.

PERSONAL LEARNING ACTIVITY 22
Write a paragraph explaining how striving has contributed to your growth as a Christian. Identify at least two specific instances of striving. Explain why these experiences were particularly difficult for you and how you ultimately benefited from the experience.

SUMMARY

Some Christians have flirted with the one-sided idea that God alone does all for man. It is true that God has provided our salvation, has enabled us to receive it, and has given us strength in living it. Nevertheless, we are responsible to cooperate with God. People do have a responsibility in the striving of the Christian life. Just as always being up makes us proud and bored, always being displaced by the Spirit denies our distinctiveness and the individuality God has given us. We strive in the power of the Spirit, but we are still here. When we are filled with the Spirit, it is we ourselves who are filled. God's Spirit does not seek to displace us. He wants to enhance us. It is the gift of the Spirit that enables us to present to God our own distinctive, best selves. God has given us only one specialized gift: the individuality of each self. He does not want to override that self in such a way as to destroy it. God's grace does not override the individuality of the created order. It brings it to its intended fullness, and this fullness involves the integrity of each individual thing that God has created. Well-meaning Christians who urge us to stop striving need to reflect on three things. (1) Striving is an inevitable part of life. (2) Christians do not strive alone. They strive with Christ and in the power of the Holy Spirit. (3) God's striving with us is designed to fulfill us, not to overwhelm us. Just as God will not permit sin to overwhelm his creation, he also does not intend that grace should do so.

The discussion is approaching full cycle. We began with what mankind was intended to be (chaps. 1 and 2). We have described mankind as it actually is (chaps. 3 through 8). One act remains. What will mankind be ultimately? The age of innocence and the age of responsibility must be rounded out by some affirmations about the age of fulfillment.

NOTES

1. John Bunyan, *The Pilgrim's Progress.* A classical mystical expression of the soul's search for and walk with God is found in the writings of St. John of the Cross, originally written in Spanish, *The Complete Works of St. John of the Cross, Doctor of the Church,* 2 vols., trans. P. Silverio de Santa Teresa, C. C., ed. E. Allison Peers (Westminster, Md.: Newman Book Shop, 1945).

2. See J. S. Whale, *Christian Doctrine* (Cambridge: University Press, 1949), pp. 75–76.

3. From *The New English Bible.* © The Delegates of the Oxford University Press, and the Syndics of the Cambridge University Press, 1961, 1970. Reprinted by permission.

4. Alex Haley, *Roots* (Garden City, N.Y.: Doubleday and Co., Inc., 1976).

5. See A. H. Strong, *Systematic Theology* (New York: A. C. Armstrong & Son, 1890), pp. 207–8.

6. See George Eldon Ladd, *A Theology of the New Testament* (Grand Rapids: Wm. B. Eerdmans Publishing Co. 1974), pp. 288–92; and W. F. Howard, *Christianity According to St. John* (Philadelphia: The Westminster Press, 1946), pp. 77 ff.

7. See George Eldon Ladd, *ibid,* pp. 511–12; and Hermann Ridderbos, *An Outline of Pauline Theology* (Grand Rapids: Wm. B. Eerdmans Publishing Co., 1975), pp. 214–23.

HANG
IN
THERE,
BABY
Is
There
Life
After
Death
?

Part 3

The Age of Fulfillment

Introduction to Part 3
The Age of Fulfillment

I have chosen to describe mankind in three phases. Essential man was a discussion of what man was intended to be. We need the age of innocence to enable us to see the deficiencies of our actual existence. And only by paying careful attention to the intentions of God for persons expressed in the concept of original man can we adequately describe what is right and what is wrong with mankind as it actually exists.

The age of responsibility is the second section of the book. It described our existence as lived. There emerged from that discussion the vital truths that we were both responsible and helpless. In the actual conditions of our existence there also emerged the good news of our redemption. There is one who is responsible for us, and there is one who helps us. It is no surprise that it is the same God who set up the intention of what mankind should be and has moved to bring all of his creation to what he desires it to be.

This third section is necessary to complete the story. This section deals with the age of fulfillment. In this final chapter we must gather up the loose ends and ask where and how it is all moving. A study of the end of things is called *eschatology*. Phase one of our study was *essential man*. Phase two was *existential man*. Phase three is *eschatological man*. In the essential stage of innocence, unfallen man was able not to sin or to die. He could choose freely, and he chose wrongly. In the existential stage of man, he is not able not to sin and to die; that is, he must sin, and he must die. In the eschatological phase, redeemed mankind will not be able to sin or to die. That is a happy destiny. If we put the three phases of the Christian view of man on a chart, they would look something like the illustration.

This threefold division of the Christian discussion of mankind is an old one going back to the fifth century. It still seems to be a very perceptive way of describing our destiny.

In phase three we ask about the outcome of mankind. Chapter 9 will describe the destiny of the individual and explore the destiny of the race and of the cosmos. Just as we began with the

PHASE ONE	**Essential Man**	**The Age of Innocence**	**Mankind is able not to sin or to die.**
PHASE TWO	**Existential Man**	**The Age of Responsibility**	**Mankind is not able <u>not</u> to sin and to die. He does sin; he must die.**
PHASE THREE	**Eschatological Man**	**The Age of Fulfillment**	**Redeemed mankind is not <u>able</u> to sin or to die.**

interwoven relationship of the one and the many, we must conclude in that same vein. In chapter 9 our major topics will be death and destiny. We will have to discuss what it means that the goals of existence are fulfilled or unfulfilled. We must explore also to what extent the intention of God for his creation is frustrated or fulfilled.

There are several guidelines or presuppositions I will use in this discussion. They are important. The reader who wants more than I will say needs to reread these presuppositions carefully.

1. I can say no more about the specifics of mankind's and the cosmos' ultimate destiny than that which the biblical materials specifically teach.
2. I do not feel that the Bible presents one complete systematic system of the last things. There are no contradictory teachings in the Bible about God's ultimate purpose. But there are likewise no complete blueprints so that all mys-

tery is removed from what is properly God's own activity.

3. I assume that all language is symbolic.
   a. Common symbols can express what all people experience. For example, death is a common symbol that all persons can understand.
   b. Technical symbols grow out of the concerns of a special group or study. For example, soul sleep is a religious term that suggests there is an unconscious state of individuals after death. I do not affirm soul sleep, but I understand what theologians who use the term mean.
   c. Poetic symbols are ways of describing reality that grows out of reality, but they cannot exhaust that reality, because the reality is greater than words can describe. An example of a poetic symbol is to speak of heaven with streets of crystalline gold and gates of pearl. It seems to me that these poetic symbols are striving to describe a reality that human words cannot exhaust.
4. To say that a thing is symbolic is not to deny that it is real. A symbolic thing is so intensely real that human words cannot describe it fully.
5. The borders beyond man's own historical experience, such as the ultimate beginnings and the ultimate conclusion of all things, are described in particularly symbolic language. This is true because no one of us has ever actually lived under those conditions, and we cannot describe them fully yet.
6. There is a difference between God's eternal dimensions and our historical dimension. God can move freely into our dimension because he is Lord of both eternity and history. But we, who are bound by history, cannot participate fully in his dimension of eternity until he permits us to do so.
7. To suppose that we have exhausted God's eternal dimension of existence by our historical description of it removes all mystery from faith and draws God's eternity into our realm of historical, scientific proof or disproof. I do not feel that we we can rob faith of its mystery by our suppositions that we have described fully God's eternity in terms of our own history.

Covering all of our discussions in this third phase of the book is Paul's reverent awareness that in our present existence "we see through a glass, darkly" (1 Cor. 13:12).

My major concern is what is the end and fulfillment God desires for his creation. He has given us some convincing promises about this; they are enough for me. I will seek to answer two major questions in chapter 9: What is God's purpose for mankind? What is the conclusion of the whole matter?

PERSONAL LEARNING ACTIVITY 23

Review the seven guidelines or presuppositions you have just studied. Make notes in the margin to indicate (1) the ones with which you agree, (2) the ones that are a new idea to you, and (3) the ones with which you disagree and why.

Chapter 9

God's Purpose for Mankind

A poster on the back of my office door is a combination of funny and encouraging. It shows a small kitten hanging desperately on a chinning bar. The legend says, "Hang in there baby!"

Many experiences in Christian existence are at best a hanging-in-there until we attain our final state or until God terminates the age. There is also a provocative poster that asks, "Is there life before death?" This is an ultimate question. And the Christian faith has some important answers to it. In Jesus Christ there is the possibility of a vibrant, beautiful existence in this world, and there is also life after death.

There is an inherent tendency in people to want to know how things come out. This tendency is not of itself bad. The desire to see the conclusion of a thing that affects our own life is natural. It is part of the goal orientation that is the genius of mankind. An ancient proverb says that God has written eternity in our hearts. This means not only that we look beyond ourselves to God, it also means that we look to God to discern what lies beyond for us. I do not fully agree with Aristotle that the end of a thing determines its worth. But I would assert that the purpose of a thing should determine its use. There should be a correspondence between what mankind is intended to be and what we ultimately become.

THE PURPOSE

The Scriptures are indirect but clear about what mankind's purpose is. From this purpose and from an awareness of God's persistence in accomplishing his purpose, we can draw an extended line to what we shall be. There is a discernible relationship between Genesis and the Gospel of John.[1] Both speak of beginning. Genesis speaks of the light of creation. John speaks of the light of redemption. Genesis declares that God made all things good in his original creation. The Gospel of John declares that God is making all things new and good in Jesus Christ. The book of the Revelation, with its Johannine insights, extends the parallel with its insistence on a new heaven and a new earth.

To arrive at a statement of God's purpose for mankind, consider the following parallel and complementary insights in Genesis and John. Genesis declares the following: God made all things. He gave them life. He declared them good. He gave mankind the option to persist in goodness and to superintend the goodness of all creation. But mankind chose to deny his responsibility, and in his refusal and rebellion the entire cosmos suffers. Mankind is excluded from the tree of life, and death is his punishment for sin. John declares the following: The whole world does lie in the power of the evil one. But God who made the world through his Word, Jesus Christ, sends the Word among us to bring the light of salvation. The light of salvation has begun to shine, and it is overcoming darkness. Jesus is sent to destroy the works of the devil. One of the principle works of the evil one is death. Christ overcomes death by his death which is a historical completion of what he came to do. His purpose was to bring life and to bring it more abundantly. The more abundant life that Christ brings to God's creation is an eternal life which is the highest and final gift of God to the world that he loves (John).

From this biblical collage, I would conclude that *God's purpose for mankind is to secure our intended goodness and the fulfillment of our life within the bounds of freedom, which he has given and by the grace he has expressed in Jesus Christ.* The gospel proclaims with magnificent regularity that God intends the good of his creation. What God began as Creator, he fulfills as Redeemer. The limitation he apparently has set for himself and mankind is the limitation of freedom, which both guarantees a free response and permits the possibility of rejection. Christians may comfort themselves and all to whom they witness with the good word that God is faithful to his creation. He desires only its good. He will bring it to completion. When an individual asks about God's intentions for himself, that person must be assured that God wills goodness and fulfillment for each of us and for all of us. We must believe that God's purpose for mankind is good and not evil. Having asserted the purpose of God, it is appropriate to ask about the process which God uses to accomplish this purpose.

THE PROCESS

We have described the historical process of redemption. It is bound up with Jesus Christ's providing for us and offering to us God's acceptance. The process is effected on our part by our acceptance of God's acceptance and our striving to live in that acceptance. But at this point we are concerned with what lies beyond that historical process of salvation we are now undergoing. Our focus here is on the process whereby God accomplishes his purpose of goodness and fulfillment for the individual beyond history. The stages of this process have been described traditionally as death, life, resurrection, judgment, and our final state. I shall speak briefly about each of these based on biblical principles that we can establish. Sometimes Christians have said too much about these steps of God's process of fulfilling us. We have been guilty occasionally of saying what people want to hear. That compromises the integrity of our message.

Death

There is an old adage that speaks of a thing being as sure as death and taxes. It brings a smile. It also conveys an indisputable truth. Death is certain. It is the inevitable boundary of our historical existence. It is the way we go out of life, and it is the shadowy limit that stretches back over all our existence. We are born to die. In a previous chapter I suggested that one could see death as a blessed relief from an endless painful historical existence. But mostly death must be seen as the consequences of sin, as the intruder who calls all the meaning of life into question. So far as persons can observe from a practical standpoint, death is the end of life.

I spoke above about death in every dimension of life, and I want to reenforce that death is the experience that affects all of life completely. Spiritual death begins with our conscious rejection of God. Psychological death begins with the loss of mental awareness and concern. Physical death begins with the cessation of the heartbeat. When the process comes to its fullness, the totality and reality of death occurs. Paul rightly understands death as our last enemy. Death is also our worst enemy.

It is a paradox that accomplishment of God's purpose for the individual is through death. God brings good from evil. Through the death of Christ, he brings an end to the ability of death to destroy his creation. It is also through an individual's death that that person is able to reach God and to realize his or her fulfillment. Those who know that Christ's death has overcome the power of death need not fear their own death. In the deepest sense, we can welcome death as the indispensable doorway to fulfillment.

Life After Death

Life after death is the second phase of the individual's fulfillment. There is a problem we face because of the difference between God's eternal dimension and our historical existence. Resurrection, which is the third phase of our fulfillment, occurs at the end of the age (1 Cor. 15). But there is from our view a time gap between the death of individuals in history and the resurrection of all persons at the end of history. The Christian community has handled this time-gap problem in three ways.

1. *By asserting that the soul sleeps until resurrection.*[2]—I do not favor this view because it tends to divide man into parts and because it overlooks the biblical indications that there is conscious existence with God after death. Such indications are found in Jesus' communion and conscious presence with God (Acts 8); the logical conclusions based on the appearance of Moses and Elijah at the mount of transfiguration (Matt. 17); even the parabolic setting of the rich man and Lazarus (Luke 16:20–25); and especially Paul's assertion that to be absent from the body is to be present with the Lord (2 Cor. 5:1–8).

2. *By asserting that each person enters into the fullness of his or her own resurrection at the time of death.*[3]—I do not favor this view because it does not permit adequate expression of the resurrection at the end of the age which occurs at the coming of Jesus Christ (1 Cor. 15; 1 Thess. 4:13–17).

3. *By asserting that individuals go into the presence of God at death in a conscious existence and in some intermediate form of the total self until the completion of the self at resurrection.*—I favor this view on the basis of 2 Corinthians 5:1–6, and on the basic biblical principle that nothing exists, not even God, without some type of shape or form that is necessary to existence. The fact that God is Spirit does not mean he is a floating vapor with no form. Biblical

thought knows nothing of unshaped pure abstractions.

It is intriguing to speculate how those who enter God's eternal dimension perceive time, if they do. Hebrews 11:1 through 12:3 seems to indicate that those in the eternal realm are in some way aware of our historical arena. But this reference is designed primarily to make us aware of the seriousness of our walk in faith, rather than to describe how we are to understand activity in God's eternal order. We who stand in the historical dimension of existence are confined to the biblical reference. We cannot know how the departed perceive the historical dimension in which we live.[4]

It can be assumed from biblical expressions that those who share life after death know one another. This was so in the recognition of the risen Christ and of such persons as Moses and Elijah. The case may be argued also from the logical conclusion that God's concern for the individual is what grants individuality and worth to every person. And it does not make sense to speak of God's fulfilling a person unless he does so by affirming that person's individuality even in eternity. It goes beyond the borders of biblical teaching to describe in detail what those who have died are doing, what they look like, and so on. These kinds of questions are always raised in the midst of human loneliness and loss. But it is best to answer all such questions with the certain promise, " 'Blessed are the dead who die in the Lord' " (Rev. 14:13, RSV).

Resurrection

The third phase of God's purpose in bringing to goodness and fulfillment his creatures, mankind, is resurrection. The term *resurrection* means *to stand up* or *stand again.* Resurrection in the sense of life after death was asserted and passionately believed in by all ancient civilizations in the Near East. The Egyptian tombs of the pharaohs are eloquent monuments to man's belief in and hope for resurrection. Resurrection was denied by the Sadducees of Jesus' day, but it was passionately believed in by the Pharisees (Matt. 22:23–33; Luke 20:27–39).

The reason ancient men accepted the idea of resurrection is because it is the only possible way one can assert an existence after this life.

The basis of the Christian belief in the resurrection is the declaration and demonstration of Jesus that he is the resurrection and the life (John 11:25). Paul was correct in asserting that the basis of Christian faith is the resurrection of Jesus Christ (1 Cor. 15:13–14). The risen Christ is the first fruit of the resurrection (1 Cor. 15:20) and the only hope we have for resurrection. There is no innate immortality that persons have as a part of their own right. All possibility of life after death and resurrection rests with God. In Jesus Christ, he has promised us resurrection on the last day. John 1:12–14 asserts that the eternal life that God promises us at resurrection is now a present possession. These references serve to confirm the abiding relationship that exists between God's revelation to individuals in history and his fulfillment of our lives beyond history. From the biblical teachings on the final judgment, we assert that both the just and the unjust, both believers and nonbelievers are resurrected (John 5:28–29). Jesus' expression in Luke 14:14 about the resurrection of the just cannot be taken to prove that only the just are raised, nor can this specific passage be used to establish that there is more than one resurrection.

Those who deny a resurrection of all mankind must assert one of the following two alternatives. No one is resurrected. In this case, there is no future life for anyone. The other alternative is that only the just are resurrected, and the wicked are destroyed. This is called conditional immortality for those who accept Christ and annihilationism for those who deny Christ. The most convincing biblical teaching against these denials of the resurrection of all mankind are the teachings about judgment. The only hope for human life after death is resurrection. The only hope for human justice after death is judgment (Matt. 25:31–46; 2 Cor. 5:10).

Judgment

Persons enter into their final state through death and through judgment. The idea of final judgment does not appeal to persons, either ancient or modern. We do not want to think about a binding decision of judgment. Judgment is God's decision, not ours. It is God who is the standard for what is right and the judge of what is right. All human justice in history is provisional. It is only the hope of final justice that guarantees the reality of or the need for all human justice. To the adage that death and taxes are the only two certain things, we can add the saying that mankind has to do only two things: die and face judgment.

The term *judgment* means *to make a decision, to make a choice.* Without judgment and discrimination, good is indistinguishable from evil, and all values are without foundation. Our historical existence is full of choices and decisions. Some of these are routine and insignificant. Others are permanent and crucial. Ultimate judgment has appeared in history in the person of Jesus Christ. This means that Christ is God's basis for deciding what is good and fulfilling for his creatures. Ultimate judgments also occur beyond history in the person of Jesus Christ. This means that Christ is God's basis for deciding what is good and fulfilling for his creatures. Ultimate judgments also occur beyond history in the person of Jesus Christ. The final discrimination for what is good is Jesus Christ. This is a good word. For it is this same Jesus Christ who has assured us that God loves us and freely accepts us. It is the limitation of freedom that gives judgment both a positive and a negative possibility. The freedom of the creature is God's limitation, which he has chosen to live with. It is also the conditions under which mankind exists. The phase of our eschatological fulfillment that is called judgment is expressed in Matthew 25; Mark 13; Luke 11:31–32; Romans 14:10; 2 Corinthians 5:10; and Revelation 20. John 5:27 indicates that God has given the decision of judgment to Jesus Christ who is God's own standard of judgment upon men. Matthew 25 indicates that God judges man according to man's faithfulness in caring for what God has given him and by virtue of the mercy and grace he shows to those who need it.

Judgment is a matter of grace and freedom. Jesus Christ is God's gracious gift to men, and he is the determinant for judgment. Since Jesus offers us God's grace, he judges us with grace when we accept his grace and give evidence of that acceptance by sharing graciously with others who also need his grace. Seen in this way, judgment is grace unto grace.

Judgment is also a matter of freedom. It is God's freedom and prerogative to judge men with grace. It is man's freedom to refuse God's judgment of grace and thereby perceive judgment as rejection and wrath rather than acceptance and love. In this dual possibility of judgment lies the tragedy of hell and the fulfillment of heaven.

We must keep in mind these points about eschatological judgment:

1. Judgment in eternity is based on one's acceptance of God's acceptance through Jesus Christ.
2. God's word of judgment in Jesus Christ is a word of grace that is intended for our good and for the fulfillment of mankind.
3. An eschatological, final judgment of God is necessary to make meaningful all judgments in history and to secure justice for mankind, even beyond history.
4. Judgment is an act of grace, but it is conducted under the divinely imposed limitation of freedom. For mankind this can mean either the acceptance of God or the rejection of God.
5. Only God in Christ is Judge, and we must leave all final judgment to him alone.

The Final State

The final phase in the process in which God accomplishes the good end he desires for man is the final state. Man's final state contains a two-fold possibility, hell (the selfish final state) or heaven (the fulfilled final state).

A person's concern for self can become so obsessive that the self is all that matters. The result is a selfish final state. The theological term for selfish final state is *hell.* When concern for self is fulfilled through a life that flows out to God and to others, the result is a fulfilled final state. The theological term for a fulfilled final state is *heaven.* The reality of both states arises from three sources. (1) The Bible gives affirmations about God's confirming the direction of man's life. (2) The demands of justice would necessitate that good and evil are separated finally. (3) Genuine freedom requires the dual possibility of both acceptance and rejection.

PERSONAL LEARNING ACTIVITY 24

Recall that chapter 6 listed four pairs of qualities and that each of these work for good or evil in a person's life. These were: glorying/pride, striving/rebellion, desire/greed, and restoration/sloth. The remainder of this chapter will show that

the patterns set in motion in this life are ultimately fulfilled in eternity. Examine the chart at the end of this chapter. As you continue studying, complete the chart to show how you feel life patterns are ultimately fulfilled in eternity.

Hell.—Biblical expressions about hell are suggestive rather than exhaustive. The grim reality of being cut off from the possibility of fellowship with God and with other persons is frighteningly real. The Old Testament word *sheol* and the New Testament word *hades* convey the idea of an unseen state; that is, a place where persons are not able to function as they do in the substantial world. It is intriguing to put forth the possibility that the selfish person expresses all of his or her selfish desires, but that there is no tangible way of finding fulfillment for those desires. That would be hell indeed. There is a tantalizing aspect of the selfish pattern of life even in our historical existence. Tantalus was a legendary king who was tied to a tree and all of the things necessary for the fulfillment of his desires came before him; but just as he reached for them, they eluded him. The selfish life is a life that knows tantalization both here and hereafter.

The desires of the selfish are always unfulfilled, because they want to direct all things in toward self-gratification. Hell is an endless grasping for things we cannot have and a clutching at things we cannot keep.

A second biblical term for hell is the New Testament *Gehenna.* Its historical reference is the smoldering valley of Hinnon, just outside of Jerusalem, which was used as the city dump. Hell is indeed the slag heap of the universe. Individuals who opt for the selfish life, which keeps God out, do not fulfill their intended function, namely, to be good and to be fulfilled. Mankind's goodness and his fulfillment rest in God. To reject God is to refuse our destiny. Things that do not fulfill their intended function are discarded. So are people. The discard of hell is no callous throwing away. It represents a grievous loss for God and for man.

The biblical witness speaks of God's faithfulness and consistency to his purpose. God's faithfulness to the principle of freedom permits a loss in his creation. Hell is also loss. It is a deprivation. Just as evil is in one sense an absence of the good, even so hell is an absence of the fellowship with God. It is the deepest penalty of hell that the selfish life keeps on rejecting the love and grace of God that is extended to him until that love and grace are perceived as wrath and damnation. God pervades his entire creation. Hell does not lie outside of his permission or awareness. The separation of outer darkness is not of such nature that those turned in upon themselves can get away from God and successfully hide. God is ruler over all of his creation, and he is everywhere present to it. The separation of the damned from God is not of such a nature that God no longer knows or cares what they do. Neither is it of such a nature that the damned are no longer aware of God's love and grace. To get away from God might be a welcome reprieve for those who have made evil their good. The selfish person is made more aware of his selfishness by virtue of the never ending and never exhausted self-giving love of God. The deprivation of hell is a deprivation of the fellowship of God.

Hell is also a deprivation of the fellowship with other persons. Just as the determination of rebellion to keep God and others out in this life excludes the joy of their fellowship, so will it be in the world to come. The cozy picture of a group of organized rebels against God joining in a camaraderie in hell is a distorted view. There is no fellowship among other persons in the place of rebellion, because the center of each self is thinking only of itself. The misery and estrangement of selfish persons in this life has all of the makings of hell about it. In his play *Who's Afraid of Virginia Woolf?* Edward Albee has given a powerful dramatic portrayal of two people who are bound to one another in selfish spite. The result of their relationship is hellish. There is a discernible correlation between the life we live in history and the life we live in eternity. The wheel of sin runs its relentless course even in hell where greed brings the penalty of tantalization and rebellion brings the deprivation of fellowship.

The sin of sloth results in an endless regression. Chapter 8 indicated that striving was an inevitable and necessary part of life. If life in the eternal dimension has a correlation to our historical dimension, persons will also strive or undergo growth in the world to come. But in a condition where the possibility of good and achievement are removed, the only direction in which the motion of life will be able to flow is backward. Dante's *Inferno* describes one of the punishments of the inferno as having to wear one's face backward for all eternity. Endless regression is the condition of the selfish life, because it does not care enough to achieve a forward motion that can be accomplished only by reaching out toward others and up toward God.

The sin of pride brings the most persistent penalty of hell, the unwillingness to acknowledge our need of help. Jesus suggested that it was necessary to recognize an illness before knowing a need for help. It is the sin of pride that keeps persons from seeking or wanting the help of God in history or eternity. There is a correlation between unpardonable sin (Matt. 10:32–39) and the inevitable persistence of sin in eternity. The reason that the sin of self-righteous persons is unpardonable is because their pride places them in a condition where they neither desire nor see their need of pardon. We may surmise from the patient nature of God and the persistent nature of pride, that the reasons persons in hell do not repent is because the sin of pride prevents their doing so or even from recognizing that they need to do so. Hell continues because of the persistence of pride, not because of a vengeful nature of God. It is pride that digs the chasm between selfish persons and God and creates what C. S. Lewis provocatively calls the "great divorce."

The results of the wheel of sin extends into the endless cycle of hell. Greed results in a tantalization that knows no satisfaction. Rebellion issues in holding God and others out, which causes the deprivation of all fellowship. Sloth rejects the forward motion of achievement and ends in the backward motion of regression. Pride creates the persistent condition of neither wanting help nor seeking help and brings about the continuation of hell itself.

Hell exists because God confirms mankind's decisions; because good and evil must be separated so that justice and value can have meaning; because genuine freedom requires the dual option of both a negative and a positive response. But heaven also exists because of these reasons. And heaven is a much happier subject.

Heaven.—Heaven is the state and place in which God fulfills his purpose for his creation. Review the purpose of God for mankind stated earlier in this chapter. Although mankind has desire for fulfillment, achievement, and perfection, there is no indication that they are ever completely achieved in this life. Heaven is the condition and the place of existence where the creator's intention for his creation is fulfilled and where the longing aspirations of man, the creature, are perfected.

Even a primitive awareness of our world thinks in terms of up and down. There is an aura of mystery about the unknown that lies beyond us. The enchantment of the beyond is beautifully expressed in Psalm 8. The world view of the Old Testament conceived of the earth as a flat surface resting on the waters beneath. Over this the heavens were stretched out like a scroll. The heavens separated the waters above from the earth and contained all of the blessings that God sent to man. God opened the windows of heaven and sent rain and other blessings. God himself dwelt in the heaven of heavens or a third heaven, which lay beyond all other things. God's heaven was the highest dimension, the final state and place which man could conceive. Modern man with his astrophysics and space explorations may tend to smile at this poetic expression of existence, but it contains two profound insights. It is important to think of some final dimension that we are unable to see with any physical instrument. And it is appropriate to think of God as over us and beyond us, as well as in our world. In the Bible, heaven is the dwelling place of God. This means that his ultimate reality lies beyond our own dimension of time and space.

For the Christian, heaven is given an added dimension as the place of Jesus Christ. Paul spoke of Christ's descending from heaven (Eph. 4:9–10). The ascension of Christ, recorded in Acts 1:9–12, is the taking of Christ into heaven. Christ now is in heaven, until the time of the restitution of all things (1 Cor. 15). It is from heaven that Christ will return (Acts 1:11; 1 Thess. 4:16). The book of Hebrews stresses that Christ has passed into the heavens to serve as our High Priest (Heb. 4:14). John records a promise that Jesus is in his Father's house preparing a place for his disciples. And it is from the Father's house that he returns to gather his disciples to himself and to welcome them into the Father's house (John 14:1–6). Heaven has played a very significant role in Christian history and art. The fullest biblical expression about heaven is in Revelation 21:10 to 22:5. In this marvelous passage of poetic symbols, there is a description that strains at the limitations of language. A threefold symbolism is in these chapters. Heaven is likened to the ancient tabernacle of God which was placed in the midst of the children of Israel. This is a symbol of God's presence. Heaven is like a walled city, which symbolizes God's protection. The third symbol of heaven is a garden where the trees produce both food for sustenance and medicinal leaves for the healing of the nations. This is a symbol of provision.[5]

Earlier in this book I have expressed some principles about man and his destiny that I would now like to use to draw out the significance of heaven. Let me review these affirmations at this point. Man's source is God and his destiny is God. God created man good, but mankind chose to do that which was less than good. The sin which man commits is inevitably woven with the possibility of his goodness. Striving is an essential movement of life. A satisfactory understanding of heaven should draw answers from the biblical materials that will correspond to these affirmations.

Since man's source and destiny is God, he must look for both the ground of his being and the end of his being in God. Since heaven is the place of God and eternity is God's time, man's search for God and his own roots finds its fulfillment in heaven with God. The good that man loses by his sin and the completeness that he lacks because of evil are to be found and brought to completion in Jesus Christ. Just as we share corporately in the loss of goodness in the first Adam, we also share corporately in the restoration of goodness in the second Adam. In both instances individuals participate—in their lostness and in their salvation. The loneliness of selfishness fragments the individual until he is an isolated self. The unity God desires for his creation inevitably requires the concern of redeemed persons for all other persons, not merely for themselves as individuals. The isolation of hell is a sharp contrast with the corporate fellowship of heaven.

The good roots connected with man's sinful possibilities are: (1) the bringing into the self those things that give growth (the counterpart of greed); (2) the straining out of all things that hurt and destroy (the counterpart of rebellion); (3) the rhythm of rest (the counterpart of sloth); and (4) the reaching toward accomplishments that leads to perfection (the counterpart of pride). A further word is in order about these good roots that are brought to fulfillment in heaven.

Striving is a part of being alive. Movement and mobility in the sense of growth are essential in our earthly existence. God's way with mankind in history is a leading onward and upward. There is no reason why this pattern should not persist in heaven. The argument might be raised that perfection and fulfillment complete the need of striving. I feel that perfection should be understood in terms of God's dynamic movement rather than in static terms of immobility. God's kind of perfection is compatible with a continual striving and growth. The job of the striving of heaven is that all negative elements that hinder achievement are removed. This is the one meaning of Revelation 20:1–3. The growth of heaven is a dramatic contrast to the endless regression of hell.

The straining out of the things that hurt and destroy makes possible the fellowship of heaven. The conditions that make possible our fear of being hurt when we open ourselves to others are removed in heaven. This is expressed beautifully by the gates in the New Jerusalem which may safely remain open, because all of those things that can harm persons are confined (Rev. 21:25). This trusting interaction with God and other persons is what is called the unhindered fellowship of heaven. This fellowship is contrasted with the loneliness and lack of fellowship in hell.

Heaven has been described often as a place of rest. The words "O land of rest, for thee I sigh" in the gospel song "We'll Work Till Jesus Comes" is one expression Christians have used to reflect on the rest of heaven. The idea of heaven as a place of rest was particularly appealing to those times when persons' lives were full of toil and work. It is only recently that we have come into a leisure-oriented age when rest is not such an appealing idea. The idea of heaven as a place of rest certainly does not appeal to children and young people whose strength and energy seem stifled by the notion of rest. It is a matter of definition. Rest need not mean inactivity. It can mean a different type of activity, an alternating type of action we call relaxation. The book of Hebrews speaks of a sabbath rest that is laid up for the people of God (Heb. 3:11–19). The author of Hebrews is thinking in terms of God as a great economist. God once offered Israel rest in the immediate entrance into Canaan, but they refused. So God offers it again to his people through Jesus Christ.[6] The final extension of God's sabbath rest through Jesus Christ is in heaven itself.

Heaven is for reaching. Growth in heaven encourages our reaching. The accomplishments of goals and the opening of the self to larger goals is a dynamic view of perfection. When we arrive in heaven, we have arrived; but we also have not arrived in the sense that there is nothing left to reach for. Oliver Wendell Holmes' poem "The Chambered Nautilus" is a beautiful way of expressing a sense of accomplishment that leads to further accomplishments.

> Through the deep caves of thought I hear a voice that sings:—
> Build thee more stately mansions, O my soul,
> As the swift seasons roll!
> Leave thy low-vaulted past!
> Let each new temple, nobler than the last,
> Shut thee from heaven with a dome more vast,
> Till thou at length art free,
> Leaving thine outgrown shell by life's unresting sea![7]

A biblical reference that may be used to express the growing sense of accomplishment is 1 Corinthians 15:24–25. The meaning of Christ yielding up the kingdom to the Father so that God might be all in all is much disputed. I see the passage as implying that Jesus continues his work and the accomplishment of his tasks to their satisfactory conclusion. The accomplishment of Christ is to perfect the people of God. The accomplishment of the people of God is to praise him who perfects them.

There is a great wisdom in the answer given in the *Westminster Shorter Catechism* about man's purpose.

> What is the chief end of man?
> Man's chief end is to glorify
> God and to enjoy him forever.[8]

Our study of the age of fulfillment is most beneficial, when we realize that it provides motivation for our lives in the present. A vision of our ultimate destiny should be used to help our present performance.

THE CONCLUSION OF THE MATTER

Where will it all end? In him with whom it all began. Mankind is a part of creation, and we are vitally related to all of the rest of creation. We are physical and bound up with the structure of existence—the laws of God. As biochemical, we are related to all matter. We are psychical, and as such we are related to all persons whose special privilege it is to reflect. We are spiritual; and because of the image of God in us, we are related to God who lies beyond us. Innocence is the essence of original creation; finitude and sinfulness are the conditions of our actual existence. The growing perfection of redeemed creation is our eschatological destiny. I have spoken of that destiny in terms of the individual. Some concluding words about the fullness and totality of God's redemptive purpose are now appropriate.

Full Circle

At various points in the book, the idea of completeness has been stressed. Robert Browning's poetry "on earth the broken arcs, in heaven the perfect whole"; Kant's philosophical requirement for eternity to complete the demands of history; Augustine's theological expression that we are not complete until we find our rest in God; and even the old gospel song "Will the Circle Be Unbroken?" all point to a common need. It is the need for a goal, a finish line, the conclusion of a thing begun. The biblical way of expressing this drive toward the goal is simple and beautiful. The great affirmation of God the Creator is the solemn and joyful word of God the Redeemer. "Behold, I make all things new" (Rev. 21:5). The newness of the end differs from the newness of the beginning. God created everything out of nothing. God will recreate everything out of his first creation which became imperfect. This recreation gives evidence of the faithfulness of God to his creation. This recreation also gives hope to a creation that has no other ultimate source of help.

Many different words or phrases are used to express the ending of a job. In the printing business the phrase is used "putting it to bed." Merchants speak of "closing time." The C.B. radio subculture closes a communication with "10–4." Note how all human endeavors have some way of expressing the necessity of a conclusion. The conclusion of the cosmos lies solely in the hands of God. Human history gives evidence that it is a long and arduous journey. I was reared in Kansas. The state motto for Kansas expresses the struggle toward statehood of that midwestern territory. The motto is "Ad Astera per Aspera"—to the stars through difficulty. That is the story of our individual redemption, and that is the story of cosmic redemption. It is a story of a grace. A favored gospel song expresses it well.

> Thro' many dangers, toils, and snares,
> I have already come;
> 'Tis grace hath bro't me safe thus far,
> And grace will lead me home.

The journey is from the high plateau of innocence (represented by the figure of unfallen Adam) to the low places of our struggling existence (represented by all of us—the children of Adam) to the fullness of perfection (which God has prepared for those who love him).

It must be said with great sorrow that not all of the creation participates in the completion of perfection. Rebellious men and spirits who have said no to God's yes in Jesus Christ remain unfulfilled and incomplete. But we may not assert from this rejecting portion of God's creation that God has failed to accomplish his purpose. He has willed the salvation of all. But his willing has included the freedom that makes the rejection of some possible. We must not place even the rejecting part of creation outside of the circle that is the purpose of God. There is an inclusion of rejection. In the last day, God excludes evil from his creation so that it can no longer distort it. But he continues to face his rejecting creatures in such a way that he also feels the pain of their rejection and his extended, but ever rejected love, increases the problem of their rejection. Hell is an exclusion from the fellowship of God and from the possibility of disrupting good. It is not, however, a getting away from God. There is no separate circle outside of God's permission where a part of his creation may do as it wishes. God is Lord of all creation, even that portion of it he created as the place of confinement of evil.

We cannot say that God has pleasure in the death of the wicked (2 Pet. 3:9). We know that God suffers with his historical creation (for example, Hosea's passionate pleas related to Israel's disobedience and God's anxiety). Jesus was justly prophesied to be and was known as a man of sorrow and acquainted with grief (Isa. 53:3). From this biblical evidence and the basic supposition that the eternal God is the same as the God we know in history, we must conclude that he also suffers with those who suffer because of their rejection of him.

To portray God any other way is to deny his goodness and compassion. All talk of hell that sounds happy because other people are getting their "just deserts" is not godly talk. In fact, all delight-in-hell talk distorts the nature of God. To know that he includes in his suffering the suffering of the rejecting is to know that he is true to his nature of suffering love. God is great enough to endure the contradiction of a part of his creation. He is just enough to separate good and evil. And he is powerful enough to secure what he has begun in Jesus Christ. What he has begun in Jesus Christ is the bringing of all creation back to himself. The conclusion of the matter is a full circle. In the closing of that circle, God completes the plan—from innocence to perfection.

The Homecoming

Homecoming is a custom people everywhere enjoy. There is the pageantry of a triumphal homecoming for a hometown hero or heroine who has "made it good." There is the delight of a whole town or city having a homecoming day for those who have moved elsewhere. There are the college and high-school homecomings for all who have "suffered" the experience of education together. Churches have homecomings complete with "dinners on the ground" to renew the fellowship of believers. And families have homecomings called reunions to draw loved ones together, to talk of memories from the past, and note the growth of children. Heaven is homecoming. There is the triumphal returning hero. There is the drawing together again of friends. There is family reunion.

The context of the homecoming of God for his creation is his new creation. This will put an end to our ideas that God redeems only persons. God loves the whole world, and it is the whole world he will save. Nothing that God has created, except rebellious men and spirits, will fail to fulfill the purpose for which it was created. This is called cosmic redemption.

The principle biblical passages that speak of cosmic redemption are:

> For the creation waits with eager longing for the revealing of the sons of God; for the creation was subjected to futility, not of its own will but by the will of him who subjected it in hope; because the creation itself will be set free from its bondage to decay and obtain the glorious liberty of the children of God. We know that the whole creation has been groaning in travail together until now; and not only the creation, but we ourselves, who have the first fruits of the Spirit, groan inwardly as we wait for adoption as sons, the redemption of our bodies (Rom. 8:19–23, RSV).

> He is the image of the invisible God, the first-born of all creation; for in him all things were created, in heaven and on earth, visible and invisible, whether thrones or dominions or principalities or authorities—all things were created through him and for him. He is before all things, and in him all things hold together. He is the head of the body, the church; he is the beginning, the first-born from the dead, that in everything he might be pre-eminent. For in him all the fulness of God was pleased to dwell, and through him to reconcile to himself all things, whether on earth or in heaven, making peace by the blood of his cross (Col. 1:15–20, RSV).

> And he who sat upon the throne said, "Behold, I make all things new." Also he said, "Write this, for these words are trustworthy and true." And he said to me, "It is done! I am the Alpha and the Omega, the beginning and the end. To the thirsty I will give water without price from the fountain of the water of life" (Rev. 21:5–6, RSV).

The denial of cosmic redemption is a denial of the goodness of the created order that God originally made. A denial of cosmic redemption means that God is not faithful to his creation. History is not important if the acts of persons in history and the created order in which history takes place are not redeemed. There is an eschatological meaning to Jesus' pronouncements that God observes the fall of every sparrow and guarantees the beauty of the lilies of the field. There is a permanent message in the spiritual "He's Got the Whole World in His Hands." One theologian has described it in these words.

> Sin will have no place in the new creation . . . and with its passing there goes the real centre of all the troubles of the universe, and all the innumerable troubles of the world will disappear. The weeping of children, the heartaches of mothers, the toil of man, the needs of the hungry and the sick, the alarms of war, the groaning of creation, all the sufferings of this present world order come to an end . . . But the most important thing of all is that the curse of corruption, the world's mortality, is taken away . . .[9]

God's homecoming is a grand affair. Historical words cannot describe it adequately. The last chapters of the book of Revelation have fired Christian imagination to anticipate it. The concluding vision of the book describes a garden. In the garden is the tree of life. We may safely eat of that tree then. For the redeemed, there are no prohibitions, only the enriching provisions of God.

> Then he showed me the river of the water of life, bright as crystal, flowing from the throne of God and of the Lamb through the middle of the street of the city; also, on either side of the river, the tree of life with its twelve kinds of fruit, yielding its fruit each month; and the leaves of the tree were for the healing of the nations. There shall no more be anything accursed, but the throne of God and of the Lamb shall be in it, and his servants shall worship him; they shall see his face, and his name shall be on their foreheads. And night shall be no more; they need no light of lamp or sun, for the Lord God will be their light, and they shall reign for ever and ever (Rev. 22:1–5, RSV).

Paul said, "For now we see through a glass, darkly; but then face to face: now I know in part; but then shall I know even as I am known" (1 Cor. 13:12). Christians draw a final joy from this statement. It is the vision of God himself. The *Westminster Shorter Catechism* has summed it up beautifully. "Man's chief end is to glorify God and to enjoy him forever."[10]

And that is the conclusion of the matter.

NOTES

1. See Raymond Brown, *The Gospel of John*, Vol. 1, *The Anchor Bible Commentary*, Vol. 29 (Garden City, N.Y.: Doubleday and Co., 1966), pp. LX–LXI.

2. For an account of this view and a refutation of it see the classical but little known work of John Calvin, *An Excellent Treatise of the Immortality of the Soul* (Ann Arbor: University Microfilm Inc., 1967).

3. See Emil Brunner, *The Eternal Hope*, trans. Harold Knight (Philadephia: The Westminster Press, 1954).

4. It should be recalled that the biblical witness is built on the distinction between time and eternity. Whereas the eternal dimension comes to us by the direct intervention of God and Jesus the Word, we are not privileged to reciprocate by climbing into God's dimension or by communicating with those who are there. The strict Old Testament proscription against communicating with the dead is, at base, a guarantee of the borders between time and eternity. For a refutation of the claims of spiritualism, see Walter Martin, *The Kingdom of the Cults* (Minneapolis: Bethany Fellowship, 1968), pp. 199–212.

5. For an elaboration of these symbols, see Ray Summers, *Worthy Is the Lamb* (Nashville: Broadman Press, 1951), pp. 211–15.

6. See William Manson, *The Epistle to the Hebrew* (London: Hodder and Stoughton, Ltd., 1951), pp. 52–56.

7. Oliver Wendell Holmes, "The Chambered Nautilus."

8. *Westminster Shorter Catechism* (Richmond: John Knox Press, 1964), p. 391.

9. E. Stauffer, *New Testament Theology*, trans. John Marsh (New York: The Macmillan Co., 1955), p. 226.

10. *Westminster Shorter Catechism, op. cit.*

How is the positive aspect of this life pattern fulfilled in heaven?	Life Pattern	How is the negative aspect of this life pattern fulfilled in hell?
	GLORYING/PRIDE	
	STRIVING/REBELLION	
	DESIRE/GREED	
	RESTORATION/SLOTH	

Small Group Study Guides

Bill Latham

SESSION 1

Introduction and Chapters 1 and 2

Training goal: By the end of this session, members (1) should have made a list of insights and/or facts that help them gain a Christian understanding of man and (2) they should have worked together to write a paraphrase of Romans 5:12–21 or 1 Corinthians 15:20–28 that expresses clearly what they feel to be the reason persons sin.

Before the Study

- Have a chalkboard or sheets of newsprint available.
- Have copies of *The Doctrine of Man* available.
- Prepare six session posters as illustrated.
- Prepare the four following group work assignment slips: *Slip 1*—Be prepared to report to the group how the relation of time and eternity helps us gain a Christian understanding of man. Use "The Relation of Time and Eternity" in chapter 1 as your resource. *Slip 2*—Be prepared to report to the group how the relation of faith and history helps us have a Christian understanding of man. Use "The Relation of Faith and History" in chapter 1 as your resource. *Slip 3*—Be prepared to report to the group how the relation of Adam to all men helps us have a Christian understanding of man. Use "The Relation of Adam to All Men" in chapter 1 as your resource. *Slip 4*—Be prepared to report to the group how the relation of innocence and perfection helps us have a Christian understanding of man. Use "Innocence Versus Perfection" in chapter 1 as your resource.
- Prepare eight flash cards as illustrated.

During the Study

- Register members as they arrive. Give each person who does not already have one a copy of *The Doctrine of Man* with instructions to review the Introduction and chapters 1–2 and complete Personal Learning Activity 5.
- Begin the session by getting acquainted. If the group is

Session 1

Introduction
Chapters 1 and 2

(Write Session 1 training goal here.)

Session 2

Chapters 3 and 4

(Write Session 2 training goal here.)

Session 3

Chapter 5

(Write Session 3 training goal here.)

Session 4

Chapter 6

(Write Session 4 training goal here.)

Session 5

Chapters 7 and 8

(Write Session 5 training goal here.)

Session 6

Chapter 9

(Write Session 6 training goal here.)

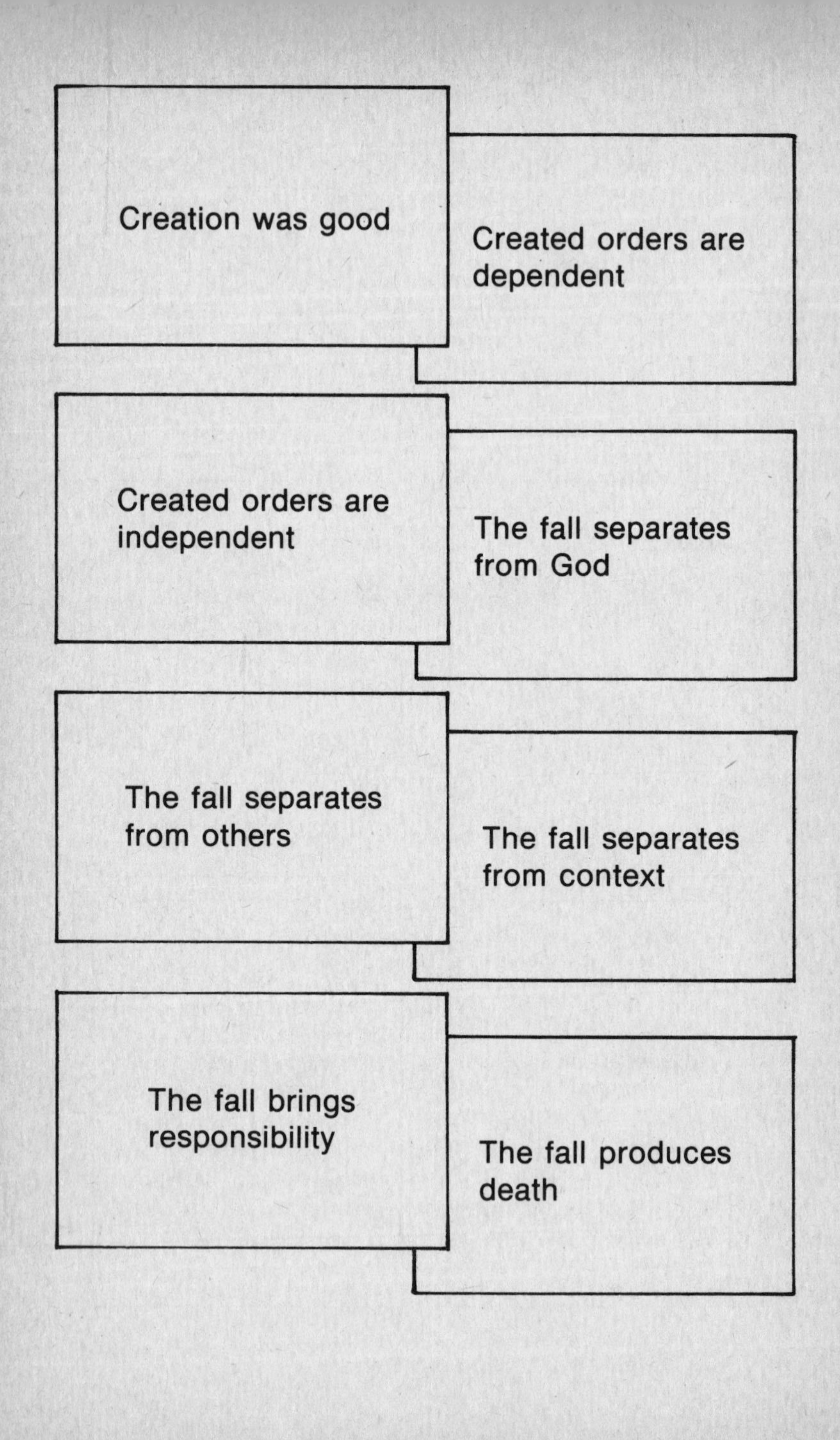
Creation was good
Created orders are dependent
Created orders are independent
The fall separates from God
The fall separates from others
The fall separates from context
The fall brings responsibility
The fall produces death

newly organized, it may be necessary to introduce members to one another. Explain that study course credit can be earned for this study and explain the requirements for earning credit. You will find an explanation of the requirements at the end of the book.

• Give an overview of the entire study. Have members turn to the table of contents. As you point out each chapter title, give a brief summary statement about that chapter. You will find one group of summary statements in the Introduction to the book. Then use the session posters to explain (1) how this study will proceed, (2) the chapters to be covered in each session, and (3) the training goal for each session.

• Explain that the purpose of the next activity is to lead members to make a list of insights and/or facts that help them gain a Christian understanding of man. Ask members to read Psalm 8. Then ask: Who is man? What does the Bible say about who man is and God's purpose for him? Allow a few minutes for members' responses. State that chapter 1 gives several clues that help us gain a Christian understanding of who man is. Ask members to recall as many of these clues as possible. Form four work groups. Give each group one of the group work assignment slips. Inform the groups that they will have ten minutes to work before reporting. If a chalkboard is not available, fasten several sheets of newsprint to the wall while the groups work. After ten minutes call for reports from the groups. Then ask members to suggest facts and/or insights that help them gain a Christian understanding of man. List their responses on the chalkboard or on newsprint.

• Use a brief lecture to summarize the following sections in chapter 2: "Creation from a Common Hand," "Created Orders—Dependent and Independent," and "'He Saw Us Ruined in the Fall.'" As you lecture, use the flash cards you have prepared.

• Ask members to read Romans 5:12–21 and 1 Corinthians 15:20–28. Comment on the reality of the fact that all persons do sin. Ask, Why is it inevitable that persons sin? Allow time for responses. Ask some members who completed Personal Learning Activity 5 to share their work with the group. Have members review "Adam Didn't Make Me Do It" and "Then Why Do People Sin?" in chapter 2. Lead members to work together to write a paraphrase of either Romans 5:12–21 or 1 Corinthians 15:20–28. This paraphrase should express clearly what group members feel to be the reason persons sin.

• Show again the session poster for this session. Call attention to the training goal and review the work done during the session. Show the session poster for session 2. Make a brief statement about the next session's study and encourage members to study chapters 3–4 before the next session.

SESSION 2

Chapters 3 and 4

Training goal: By the end of this session, members should have stated how the elements of personhood have been important in their own lives. They also should be able to explain in their own words what it means to be created in the image of God and what sin has done to that image.

Before the Study

• Prepare four sheets of newsprint as illustrated and fasten them to the wall in different parts of the room.

• Have the session poster for this session on hand.

• Have pencils available.

• Have several concordances available.

• Enlist a member in advance to explain how fallenness is a denial of responsibility and how that fall has marred the image in which we were created. This explanation should include a definition of total and partial depravity. The true meaning of total depravity should be emphasized.

During the Study

• Ask members as they arrive to read Romans 7—8 and complete Personal Learning Activity 6. If necessary, allow this activity to continue several minutes into the session time. While members work, check attendance, register new members, and give them copies of *The Doctrine of Man.*

• To begin the study, show the session poster for this session and call attention to the training goal. Then use the introductory material in chapter 3 to introduce the next activity. Lead up to a

What have you achieved through human labor that has caused you to feel more fulfilled as a person? What part did God play in that achievement?

What can you do to (1) strengthen in your life the rhythm of work/play, (2) make your work a greater source of joy, and (3) find more joy and excitement in your worship?

How are thinking and reasoning consistent with the Holy Spirit's leadership in your growth as a person?

For you, what is real worship?

point at which you emphasize the dividing forces that operate in a person. Then ask some who completed Personal Learning Activity 6 to share their work with the group.

• Ask members to recall and discuss the four ideas used to express personhood (man the worker, man the player, man the thinker, and religious man). As each is discussed, lead members to consider how that quality is important to personhood, completeness, and fulfillment and how God intends man to use that quality for his own good. Call attention to the sheets of newsprint fastened to the wall. Read the questions written on each. Distribute pencils to members who need them. Declare a ten-minute work break during which members will work informally. Each member should go to as many sheets of newsprint as he wishes. On each sheet he should write one or two sentences that express his answer to the questions written on the newsprint.

• Ask members to work individually to complete Personal Learning Activity 10. Distribute concordances to those who need them. After several minutes ask some members to share their work with the group. Then compare members' answers with the definition of image and likeness given in chapter 4. Lead members to discuss the author's definition. How does the author's definition differ from members' definitions? Ask members if they can accept the author's definition. If they can, why? If they cannot, why not?

• Call on the member enlisted to present information about fallenness. Then lead members to discuss the information presented.

• Ask members to read together the Scripture passages referred to in "The True Image" in chapter 4 and discuss how Christ is the one ideal that illustrates what the image of God in man ought to be and is ultimately going to be.

SESSION 3

Chapter 5

Training goal: By the end of this session, members should be able to define *body, soul, spirit,* and *flesh* and explain how each is related to the total person. They also should have listed actions your church can take to help others find full salvation.

Before the Study

• Have copies of *The Doctrine of Man* available.

• Have the session poster for this session available.

• Enlist a member to explain the two-part view of persons and point out why that view is unsatisfactory. This person should use "The Angel in the Slot Machine" in chapter 5 as a resource.

• Enlist four members for advance assignments if you choose the alternate activity.

During the Study

• As members arrive, ask them to review chapter 5 and complete Personal Learning Activity 13. While members work, register new members and check attendance.

• Use the introductory paragraphs in chapter 5 to introduce this session. This introduction should call attention to the terms that will be studied (body, soul, spirit, flesh) and should emphasize that these are interrelated parts of the total person. Show the session poster for this session and explain the training goal.

• Call on the person enlisted in advance to explain the two-part view of persons.

• Lead members in a study and discussion of the meaning of body. Encourage members to use their Bibles and to discuss the meaning of Scripture passages referred to in "Body" in chapter 5. Fasten a large sheet of newsprint to the wall and write *Body* at the top. Lead the group to decide on a definition of body and write that definition on the top half of the newsprint. Use "Body" in chapter 5 as your resource for this activity. A Bible dictionary and commentaries also will be helpful. If possible, borrow these from your pastor or from your media center (church library).

• Follow the same procedure to discuss and define soul, spirit, and flesh.

• *Alternate activity:* You may wish to enlist four group members to lead the preceding activity. If you choose to do this, assign one term to each member. You should make available to each person a Bible dictionary and commentaries for preparing the assignment.

• After the four definitions have been written on newsprint, lead members to discuss how each is a part of the total person. Lead members to discuss also how each is related to and dependent on the other three.

• Ask, When we consider this view of personhood, what does God save when he saves us? Allow time for members' responses and discussion. Attempt to lead members in their discussion to see that salvation involves the total person.

• Call attention to the term *full salvation* that begins the final section in chapter 5. Ask members to discuss what they feel the term means. Fasten two sheets of newsprint to the wall. At the top of one write *Already Doing*. At the top of the other write *Could Begin Doing*. Ask, What is our church doing now to help others find full salvation? Write members' responses on the first sheet of newsprint. Ask, What could our church begin doing to help others find full salvation? Write members' responses on the second sheet of newsprint.

SESSION 4

Chapter 6

Training goal: By the end of this session, members should have written definitions of evil and of sin. They should be able to explain in their own words the difference between evil and sin. They should be able to recall four aspects of sin and explain how each affects a person's life.

Before the Study

• Have the session poster for this session on hand.

• Enlist three members for a panel discussion. Give panel members a list of the questions they will discuss. Emphasize that all panel members are to be prepared to discuss all the questions.

• Place at the front of the room a table and chairs for the panel.

• Have pencils and paper on hand.

• Prepare four posters as illustrated.

During the Study

• Check attendance as members arrive. Ask members to begin reviewing chapter 6.

• Use the introductory material in chapter 6 and the session poster to introduce the study.

• Explain to members that they will hear a panel discuss the meaning of sin and the meaning of evil. Ask them to listen and make notes so they will be prepared to ask questions and to discuss what panel members have said. Alert members that later in the session each person will write a definition of evil and a definition of sin.

• Introduce the panel members and seat them at the front of the room. Use the following questions to moderate a discussion of evil and sin. As you lead the discussion, see that different panel members are given an opportunity to answer or comment about each question you ask.

—What is the difference between evil and sin?

—If you had to give a one-sentence definition of evil, what would it be?

—If you had to give a one-sentence definition of sin, what would it be?

—If God is good and all-powerful, why does he permit evil when he could prevent it?

—If God is good, how can he allow evil to harm those he loves, especially if he has the power to prevent it?

—How do you feel about the solution some have offered that God is not really all-powerful or that evil does not really exist?

—Is it possible that God permits evil to exist in order to teach us a lesson?

—It appears that we must eventually come to the point of saying we do not know why evil exists or what purpose it serves. What hope or what resources do we have to help us live with the reality of evil?

—What is the danger of defining sin with a list of do's and don'ts?

—On one hand, we point out the danger of defining sin with a list of do's and don'ts. On the other hand, we know that we must be specific about sin and sinfulness. What is the balance between being specific and allowing our lists of do's and don'ts to turn us into legalists?

After the panel discussion, allow members to ask questions and discuss ideas presented by panel members.

Pride

REBELLION

SLOTH

GREED

• Ask members to recall the four aspects of sin that are discussed under "The Roots of Sin and Achievement Are Interwoven" (pride, rebellion, greed, sloth). Show the poster for pride. Ask, How does this poster illustrate the way pride operates in a person's life? Lead members to discuss the effect of pride in a person's life. Comment that chapter 6 points out that the positive aspect of pride can be helpful to a person's life. Ask members to recall what the positive aspect is and how it can be helpful.

• Follow the same procedure to discuss rebellion, greed, and sloth.

• Distribute pencils and paper to group members. Ask each person to write a definition of evil and a definition of sin. Ask members to work in groups of two or three to share and compare definitions and to discuss with one another the difference between evil and sin.

• Say: While you are working together, I want to give you one more assignment. Work together to recall the five aspects of sin. Discuss with one another how each affects a person's life and how each also has the possibility for good.

• Reserve time at the end of the session to allow members to ask and seek answers for any question that may have come up as they worked together in the previous activity.

SESSION 5

Chapters 7 and 8

Training goal: By the end of this session, each member should have written a brief testimony telling about his experience of acceptance and striving.

Before the Study

• Have session posters 1–5 available.

• Enlist a member to explain why and how persons resist God's acceptance.

• If no chalkboard is available, have newsprint.

• Have pencils and paper available.

• At the top of a large piece of poster board write *Acceptance/Striving*. Then list from chapter 8 the unsatisfactory ideas about acceptance and striving.

During the Study

- Check attendance as members arrive.
- Begin by leading a brief review of the study to this point. Use the session posters for sessions 1–4 and the information in the second paragraph under "The Proclamation of Acceptance" in chapter 7. As each session is reviewed, show its relationship to the other sessions. State that his session deals with what God does to help us in our fallenness. The terms commonly used are *justification* and *sanctification.* The author of the text uses acceptance and striving. First, God has accepted us in our fallenness and has acted to make forgiveness possible for every person. Second, a person should respond by accepting God's acceptance and by striving to be like God. Show the session poster for this session and call attention to the training goal.
- Ask members to recall the parable of the lost child that begins chapter 7 and discuss how the text compares that experience to a person's experience of salvation.
- Call on the member enlisted in advance to explain why and how persons resist God's acceptance.
- Have members read Personal Learning Activity 19 in chapter 7. Ask that each person choose one of the passages referred to, read it, and identify the major points of God's good news in that sermon. (Be certain that each reference is chosen by at least one group member.) After group members have had time to work, ask them to report the major points they identified in the sermons they studied. List their responses on a chalkboard or on a piece of newsprint fastened to the wall.
- Explain the use of the term *kerygma* in the New Testament. Lead members to recall from chapter 7 and discuss the five major points in the *kerygma.* Then compare the list in chapter 7 to the list group members have made.
- State that man's response to God's acceptance is repentance and faith. Lead members to discuss their answers to these questions: How is repentance more than an emotional experience? How is faith more than a blind act?
- Distribute pencils and paper. Ask each person to write one or two paragraphs telling about his experience of accepting God's acceptance. After members have had a few minutes to work, ask them to hold their papers and complete their testimonies later in the session.

• Point out that the text uses acceptance to express the idea of justification and striving to express the idea of sanctification. Remind members that the text stressed that in the Christian walk, the first step must be acceptance and the second striving.

• Show the acceptance/striving poster. Lead members to discuss why each idea fails to explain satisfactorily the relationship between acceptance and striving.

• Use a brief lecture to summarize information in the remainder of the chapter.

• Ask members to add one or two more paragraphs to the testimonies they began earlier. Each person should tell about his experience of striving in the Christian walk and some of the results it has produced in his life.

• Use the remaining time to allow members who wish to do so to share their testimonies with the group.

SESSION 6

Introduction to Part 3 and Chapter 9

Training goal: By the end of this session, members should be able to explain in their own words how the life patterns established in this life are ultimately fulfilled in eternity.

Before the Study

• Have the session poster for this session on hand.

• Prepare the following introductory activity assignment slips in a quantity sufficient for each member to have one: Study the seven guidelines or presuppositions in Introduction to Part 3. Beside each, write your reaction to that statement. Use agree strongly, agree, undecided, disagree, disagree strongly to indicate your reactions.

• Enlist four members to explain how death, life after death, resurrection, and judgment are a part of the process by which God brings his creation to fulfillment. Each person should note that in the third paragraph under "The Purpose" in chapter 9 the author states what he feels is God's purpose for mankind.

• Use a strip of wrapping paper or several sheets of newsprint taped together to reproduce the chart in Introduction to Part 3.

During the Study

• As members arrive, give each an introductory activity assignment slip. While members work on this assignment, check attendance. Allow this activity to continue several minutes into the session time if necessary.

• Fasten the chart to the wall. Use a brief lecture to present the information in Introduction to Part 3. As you present the seven guidelines or presuppositions, comment that it is necessary to understand that this is the perspective from which the author writes. Allow time for members to discuss whether they agree or disagree with each one.

• Ask members to recall from chapter 6 what the author feels to be God's purpose for persons. Ask: Do you agree or disagree with this statement of purpose? What, if anything, would you add or take away from the statement? Then note that chapter 9 discusses five steps in the process by which God brings his creation to fulfillment. Ask members to recall these steps. Call for reports from the members enlisted to discuss the first four of these steps. After each report give members time to discuss the information presented.

• Ask members to read again the section in chapter 9 titled "The Final State." Then lead members to work as a group to complete Personal Learning Activity 24. You should study this section very carefully as a part of your preparation to lead this activity.

• Use the information in "The Conclusion of the Matter" to conclude the study.

• Lead a brief recall review. Ask members to recall and share with the group facts they have learned or insights they have gained during this study of *The Doctrine of Man.*

• Explain again the requirements for receiving study course credit. Give make-up assignments to members who may have missed one or more sessions.

The Church Study Course

The Church Study Course consists of a variety of short-term credit courses for adults and youth and noncredit foundational units for children and preschoolers. The materials are for use in addition to the study and training curriculums made available to the churches on an ongoing basis.

Study courses and foundational units are organized into a system that is promoted by the Sunday School Board, 127 Ninth Avenue, North, Nashville, Tennessee 37234; by the Woman's Missionary Union, 600 North Twentieth Street, Birmingham, Alabama 35203; by the Brotherhood Commission, 1548 Poplar Avenue, Memphis, Tennessee 38104; and by the state conventions affiliated with the Southern Baptist Convention.

Study course materials are flexible enough to be adapted to the needs of any Baptist church. The resources are published in several different formats—textbooks of various sizes, workbooks, and kits. Each item contains a brief explanation of the Church Study Course and information on requesting credit. Additional information and interpretation are available from the participating agencies.

Types of Study and Credit

Adults and youth can earn study course credit through individual or group study. Teachers of courses or of foundational units also are eligible to receive credit. Reading the book is required for study course credit.

1. *Class experience.*—Group involvement with course material for the designated number of hours for the particular course. A person who is absent from one or more sessions must complete the Personal Learning Activities for each session missed.
2. *Individual study.*—This includes reading, viewing, or listening to course material and completing the specified requirements for the course.
3. *Lesson course study.*—Parallel use of designated study course material during the study of selected units in Church Program Organization periodical curriculum units. Guidance for this means of credit appears in the selected periodical.
4. *Institutional study.*—Parallel use of designated study course material during regular courses at educational institutions, including Seminary Extension Department courses. Guidance for this means of credit is provided by the teacher.

Credit is awarded for the successful completion of a course of study. This credit is granted by the Church Study Course Awards Office, 127 Ninth Avenue, North, Nashville, Tennessee 37234, for the participating agencies. Form 151 (available free) is recommended for use in requesting credit.

When credit is issued to a person on request, the Awards Office sends to the church two copies of a notice of credit earned. The original copy of the credit slip should be filed by the Study Course Records Librarian in the participant's record of training folder. The duplicate should be given to the person who earned the credit. Accumulated credits are applied toward leadership or member development diplomas, which are measures of learning, growth, development, and training.

Detailed information about the Church Study Course system of credits, diplomas, and record keeping is available from the participating agencies. Study course materials, supplementary teaching or learning aids, and forms for record keeping may be ordered from Baptist Book Stores.

The Church Study Course Curriculum

Credit is granted on those courses listed in the current copy of Church Services and Materials Catalog, the Church Study Course Catalog, and Baptist Book Store Catalog. When selecting courses or foundational units, the current catalogs should be checked to determine what study course materials are valid.

How to Request Credit for This Course

This book is the text for a course in the subject area Baptist Doctrine.

The course is designed for six hours of group study. Credit is awarded for satisfactory class experience with the study material for the minimum number of hours. A person who is absent for one or more sessions must complete the Personal Learning Activities for each session missed.

Credit is also allowed for use of this material in individual study and in lesson course study and institutional study, if so designated.

After the course is completed, the teacher, the Study Course Records Librarian, or any person designated by the church should complete Form 151 (Church Study Course Credit Request, Revised 1975) and send it to the Awards Office, 127 Ninth Avenue, North, Nashville, Tennessee 37234. Individuals also may request credit by writing the Awards Office or by using the special coupon on the last page of this book.

Reading the book is required for study course credit.

Cut along this line

INSTRUCTIONS: If requested by the teacher, fill in this form and give it to him when the course is completed. If preferred, mail this request for course credit to

AWARDS OFFICE
THE SUNDAY SCHOOL BOARD, SBC
127 NINTH AVENUE, NORTH
NASHVILLE, TENNESSEE 37234

State Convention | Association | Indicate Type of Study (X): ☐ Class ☐ Individual ☐ Lesson Course ☐ Educational Institution

CHURCH
- Church Name
- Mailing Address
- City, State, Zip Code

MAIL TO
- Mail to (If Different from Church Address)
- Street, Route, or P.O. Box
- City, State, Zip Code

LAST NAME	FIRST NAME AND MIDDLE INITIAL	MRS. (X)	COURSE TITLE
			The Doctrine of Man